make it count

MOVE PAST YOUR PAST AND LIVE
WITH PURPOSE TODAY

WRITTEN BY BETHANY RUTH AND BRONWYN CARDWELL

Welcome to Deuteronomy

The team dragged into the locker room. The first half of the game had been a disaster. Familiar plays had not been executed. The coach's directives had not been followed. Players had been removed from the game due to injury and penalty. Breathing hard and with heads down, the players had little hope for the second half.

Their coach entered and gathered them around. He reviewed the reality of the score, the lost players, the disregarded instructions and selfish mistakes. They could not reverse those mistakes, but they could set aside the past and play as they knew how to do. The task would not be easy, but they had what was necessary. As the coach encouraged his players, his confidence rallied the discouraged team. As he reminded them each play was a new start, his passion for their success stirred their own passion. As he challenged each one to do what was necessary, they felt hope rise within them.

Deuteronomy reads like such a story: God's people were at a key moment of transition, a turning point in their history. Up to this point in the story, things really hadn't worked out too well for the Israelites, but Moses knew their years of disobedience, failure and struggle were not the end of their story. He pointed them toward a future of obedience, purpose and victory. Like that zealous coach, Moses desired to motivate God's people to move past their past and to live with purpose in order to accomplish the goal before them.

Our lives today are not so different. We, like the Israelites, find ourselves on a journey — a journey that has, perhaps, not gone as well as we expected thus far.

Perhaps we are overwhelmed by our sin and mistakes.

Perhaps we struggle to believe God is present.

Perhaps we have even lost sight of where we are headed or lack the confidence to keep going.

Friend, this ancient book of Deuteronomy speaks directly into our lives today.

Deuteronomy will help us move past our past. Along with the Israelites, we will look back in order to reevaluate where we are headed. We will see our past through the eyes of God's inexhaustible mercy and faithfulness. As Moses challenged the Israelites with God's words of discipline and truth, we, too, will learn to listen and respond to God in faith and obedience.

Deuteronomy will help us live with purpose today. Along with the Israelites, we will seek to continue our journey with the right focus and goals. We will worship God alone and anchor our faith to His unchanging character. We will remember God's marvelous deeds so we are more aware of His presence in our every day. We will live in the freedom of the salvation He has purchased for us and walk in obedience to His commands. We will experience joy and satisfaction as we obediently fulfill all He has planned for us to accomplish for His glory.

God did not give up on His people, the Israelites, even though their sin was great, their path had wandered and their eyes were on themselves instead of on Him. And He has not given up on us. The principles of Deuteronomy will direct us through whatever temptations and battles we may yet face as we journey into the inheritance God has promised us.

Welcome to our study of *Deuteronomy*!

— BETHANY AND BRONWYN

Biblical *Context* of Deuteronomy

God's promises to Abraham

GENESIS 12

> 1. Abraham's descendants will number more than the sand of the sea or the stars of the sky.

> 2. God promises the nation of Israel a land of their very own.

> 3. All peoples on earth will be blessed through the chosen people of God, the nation of Israel.

The Israelites immediately rebel by making and worshiping the golden calf

EXODUS 32

God gives Moses the Ten Commandments and confirms His covenant with Israel

EXODUS 20-24

The Israelites arrive at Mount Sinai three months after leaving Egypt

EXODUS 19

ISRAEL LEARNS HOW TO SERVE GOD AT MOUNT SINAI, BUILDS THE TABERNACLE, RECEIVES THE LAW, CONSECRATES THE PRIESTS

God brings consequences but forgives the people and further reveals Himself to Moses

EXODUS 33-34

The Israelites follow God's instructions for building the tabernacle and it is set up 12 months after they left Egypt

EXODUS 35-40

God provides instructions for the sacrificial system so He may dwell in the tabernacle among His people

LEVITICUS 1-27

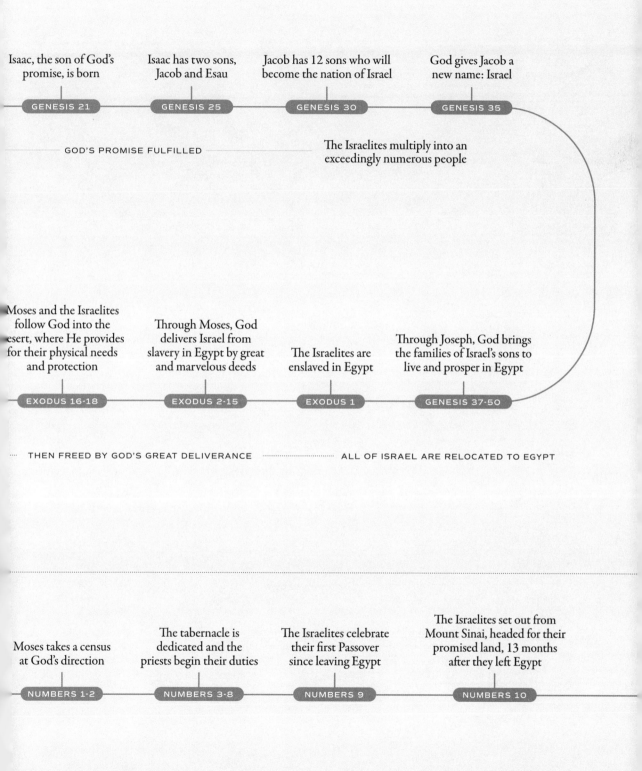

Isaac, the son of God's
promise, is born

GENESIS 21

Isaac has two sons,
Jacob and Esau

GENESIS 25

Jacob has 12 sons who will
become the nation of Israel

GENESIS 30

God gives Jacob a
new name: Israel

GENESIS 35

GOD'S PROMISE FULFILLED

The Israelites multiply into an
exceedingly numerous people

Moses and the Israelites
follow God into the
desert, where He provides
for their physical needs
and protection

EXODUS 16-18

Through Moses, God
delivers Israel from
slavery in Egypt by great
and marvelous deeds

EXODUS 2-15

The Israelites are
enslaved in Egypt

EXODUS 1

Through Joseph, God brings
the families of Israel's sons to
live and prosper in Egypt

GENESIS 37-50

THEN FREED BY GOD'S GREAT DELIVERANCE · · · · · · · · · · · · · · ALL OF ISRAEL ARE RELOCATED TO EGYPT

Moses takes a census
at God's direction

NUMBERS 1-2

The tabernacle is
dedicated and the
priests begin their duties

NUMBERS 3-8

The Israelites celebrate
their first Passover
since leaving Egypt

NUMBERS 9

The Israelites set out from
Mount Sinai, headed for their
promised land, 13 months
after they left Egypt

NUMBERS 10

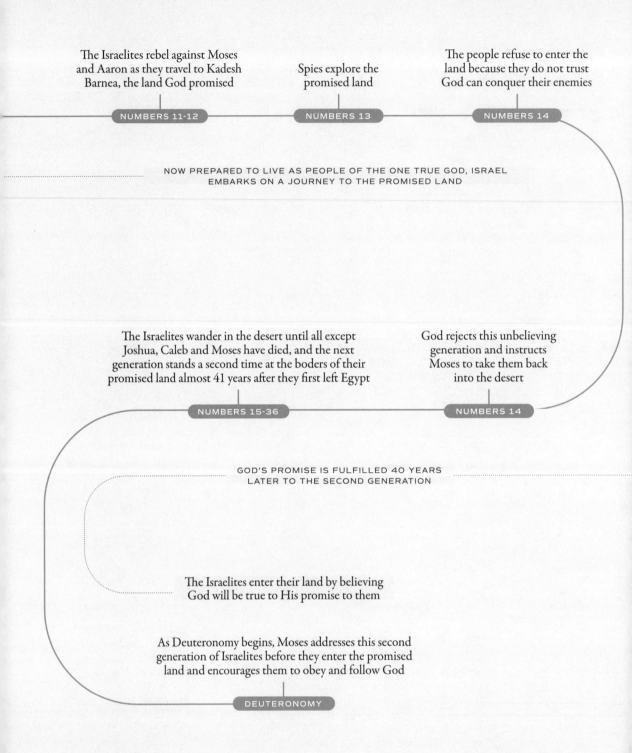

The Israelites rebel against Moses and Aaron as they travel to Kadesh Barnea, the land God promised

Spies explore the promised land

The people refuse to enter the land because they do not trust God can conquer their enemies

NUMBERS 11-12

NUMBERS 13

NUMBERS 14

NOW PREPARED TO LIVE AS PEOPLE OF THE ONE TRUE GOD, ISRAEL EMBARKS ON A JOURNEY TO THE PROMISED LAND

The Israelites wander in the desert until all except Joshua, Caleb and Moses have died, and the next generation stands a second time at the boders of their promised land almost 41 years after they first left Egypt

God rejects this unbelieving generation and instructs Moses to take them back into the desert

NUMBERS 15-36

NUMBERS 14

GOD'S PROMISE IS FULFILLED 40 YEARS LATER TO THE SECOND GENERATION

The Israelites enter their land by believing God will be true to His promise to them

As Deuteronomy begins, Moses addresses this second generation of Israelites before they enter the promised land and encourages them to obey and follow God

DEUTERONOMY

We all have a *backstory*.

Sometimes, we want people to understand where we've been, the highs and lows we've experienced, or what has shaped us into who we are. Other times, we prefer to gloss over what's in the past, thinking some realities are best kept out of sight. As we embark on our study of Deuteronomy, let's get caught up on the backstory of this wandering Israelite nation and their leader, Moses. If we can grasp their past, we'll learn more from their present challenges and their future hopes.

Where has this wandering nation of Israel come from? Their history is recorded in the first five books of the Bible.

- In Genesis, God chose one man, Abraham, through whom He would work His redeeming purposes for humanity.

- In Exodus, Abraham's descendants became the covenant nation of Israel, freed from slavery by God's great acts of deliverance, freed from bondage to a cruel master to follow a just and compassionate Master.

- In Leviticus, God taught the nation of Israel about His holiness and provided a system for them to follow so they might live as a holy people and so He could dwell among them.

- In Numbers, God moved the Israelites from theory to practice, teaching them over and over what life looked like when their actions reflected, or did not reflect, faith in His promises and belief in what He said.

- Finally, in Deuteronomy, God brought a new generation of Israelites to the border of the promised land, where Moses challenged the nation to trust and obey God and move fearlessly forward to occupy the land in faith.

Of course, this is about as simplified a look at the content of these five books as could possibly be given. For greater detail, review the timeline on pages 4-6.

This history of Israel is also *our* backstory as God's people because the Israelites are the ancestors of Jesus Christ, our Lord and Savior. God's work with Israel foreshadowed the reality of redemption that has now been completed by Jesus.

- God chose us in Christ before the world existed. (Ephesians 1:4) Our history is completely changed by Jesus Christ, through whom God worked His redeeming purposes for humanity.

- As God's redeemed people, we are now freed from bondage to the slavery of sin. By God's great act of deliverance in salvation, we have been freed from the cruel master of darkness and death in order to serve our just and compassionate Master, Jesus, in His Kingdom of light and life.

- Because God accepted the perfect holiness of Jesus' sacrifice, He has given His Holy Spirit to His people to dwell within us, providing power to live holy and obedient lives.

- God moves us from theory to practice, teaching us by His Word how to walk by faith, use the gifts of His Holy Spirit to minister within the body of Christ, and demonstrate the fruit of the Spirit as we serve those He brings across our paths.

- Finally, recognizing this world is not our home, we live with new purpose, boldly moving forward and proclaiming the Truth of our Savior so others may find His freedom and forgiveness. In faith, we wait for our promised eternal inheritance, *"undefiled, and unfading, kept in heaven for [us]"* (1 Peter 1:4).

By studying the lives and experiences of the Israelites, we will find an amazing transfer of God's truths directly into our lives as His people.

Who Wrote Deuteronomy?

Moses was God's first prophet to the nation of Israel. Throughout the books of the Torah, or the Pentateuch, God spoke His words to Moses, and Moses communicated those words to God's people and to others, like Pharaoh of Egypt. (Exodus 8:1; Exodus 35:1; Leviticus 18:1-2; Numbers 9:1-4) Deuteronomy, the fifth book of the Pentateuch, indicates Moses as the speaker: *"These are the words that Moses spoke ..."* (Deuteronomy 1:1). This is called an internal witness of authorship.

Deuteronomy contains Moses' last words to the Israelites on the plains of Moab just before Israel entered Canaan. Deuteronomy 31:9 tells us Moses not only spoke these farewell messages but also wrote them out for Israel. Scholars explain small sections of this book — for example, the passages about Moses' death and his epitaph in Deuteronomy 34 — were completed or edited by another writer, possibly Joshua. Ancient Jewish tradition also clearly identified Moses as the author of Deuteronomy.[1]

And in addition to Jewish belief and the internal witness of the book itself, the New Testament confirms Moses as the author: When responding to a Pharisee, Jesus referred to Deuteronomy 24:1-4 as the words of Moses. (Matthew 19:7-8; Mark 10:2-5) On another occasion, Jesus quoted Deuteronomy 5:16 along with Exodus 21:17 as the words of Moses, condemning the Pharisees for disregarding the commands of God they had received. Jesus' apostles also

recognized Moses as the author of this book: Paul referenced Deuteronomy 32:21 as the words of Moses, (Romans 10:19) and Peter did the same when he quoted Deuteronomy 18:15 in Acts 3:22. The author of Hebrews spoke of the "law of Moses" as he explained the danger of rejecting Jesus (Hebrews 10:28-29). When the New Testament recognizes Moses as the author of Deuteronomy, scholars call this an external witness.

Moses' voice, throughout Deuteronomy, is passionate. He loved God's people and had long walked with them. He shared their hope of entering the land God had promised. But when Moses gave these messages, he already knew he would not enter the land with the rest of Israel. (Numbers 20:1-13) Still, as their prophet and shepherd, Moses focused the attention of God's people on the riches of God's law and challenged them to follow God in faith and obedience so they would find blessing when they arrived in the promised land, Canaan.

Structure and *Form* in Deuteronomy

Deuteronomy provides theological truth packaged in multiple genres. We find narrative; history; explanation and application of Israel's laws; Moses' blessings for the nation; and even a song of catechism, which is an oral method of learning spiritual principles. The title Deuteronomy originated in the Greek: "Deuteronomy" means "the second law" or, more specifically, "the second giving of the law."[1] In truth, Moses was teaching the same law in greater depth.

This book gathers three final messages given by Moses to the people he had led for 40 years. All of Israel heard these instructions over the span of one month just before they entered Canaan.

Moses' first speech, Chapters 1-4, looked back at the Israelites' past and provided a historical review. His focus was on what God had already done for Israel and what mistakes Israel had made along their journey.

Moses' second speech was his longest, stretching from the end of Chapter 4 all the way into Chapter 26. Here, Moses' purpose was to urge the Israelites to live joyfully in covenant with their God by obeying His law. Moses reviewed the general principles of the covenant and expanded on the Ten Commandments. Because the law given in Exodus had been lived out during the nation's nomadic years, Moses gave many applications of the law for Israel's new circumstances, focusing on how the people would live when they settled in Canaan.

Moses wrapped up with a third speech in Chapters 27-33. He confirmed the covenant with the current generation of God's people and explained how God would respond to Israel's obedience or disobedience. Moses' last action before his death was to pass the torch of leadership to Joshua in the presence of all the people.

About a century ago, a flurry of scholars attempted to place the writing of Deuteronomy at a much later date in Israel's history. These ideas were based on suppositions that Moses, in the culture of his time, circa 1400 B.C., could not have created a detailed system of government and laws for the Israelites such as the book of Deuteronomy represents. Some scholars even questioned whether Moses would have been able to write.[2] They proposed Deuteronomy must have been composed in Jerusalem during the reforms of King Josiah of Israel, nearly 1,000 years later.[3]

Archaeology has since discovered numerous military documents from the time of Moses that were written in a very specific format called the Near East Suzerain Treaty Pattern. This pattern contains specific sections corresponding almost exactly to the structure of Deuteronomy.[4] Because of these artifacts, we can recognize Moses as the author of Deuteronomy with even more confidence. The structure of Deuteronomy itself provides credence that it was written during the life and time of Moses.

Ancient Treaty *Structure*	Deuteronomy
Preamble	1:1-5
Historical Prologue	1:6-4:43
General Stipulations	4:44-11:32
Specific Stipulations	12:1-26:19
Blessings and Curses	27:1-28:68
Document Clause	31:9-29
Witnesses	32:1-47

Themes in
DEUTERONOMY

These are four of the most frequent threads, or themes, God has woven into Moses' messages throughout Deuteronomy:

A UNIQUE, COVENANTAL GOD

Moses repeatedly pointed the Israelites to who God is and what He had done for them. He alone is the one true God. He is mighty in power and sovereign over the world. He is faithful to His promises, even though His people are sinful. He is merciful and gracious, overflowing with steadfast love and compassion. Again and again He forgives His people's disobedience, not treating them as their sins deserve. But He is also perfectly just and righteous to bring judgment on the unrepentant and discipline on the rebellious.

A CHOSEN, COVENANTAL PEOPLE

Moses repeatedly reminded the Israelites of who they were and of the dangers that would surround them as they moved into the promised land. Moses also encouraged the Israelites to embrace worship as God prescribed, urging them to live by faith as the foundation for holiness. He pointed out how their fathers had broken covenant with God, and he challenged the people to acknowledge their need for God. In fact, Moses' goal was to convince this second generation to recognize their weaknesses so they could avoid the problems of the first generation.

THE COVENANTAL RELATIONSHIP

Moses repeatedly challenged the Israelites to remember that how they participated in God's covenant mattered. The relationship between Yahweh and Israel was to be a relationship of love. Moses explained the consequences of forgetting God in the promised land and warned that all sin and rebellion would cause a serious breach in the covenant relationship. Moses warned God's people not to walk in idolatry, sexual immorality, unbelief or self-righteousness. He instead held out the promise of great covenant blessings if God's people would choose to walk with Him.

TRANSITION FOR THE NATION OF ISRAEL

Moses refocused the Israelites away from their past in Egypt and their past in the wilderness, and instead he pointed them toward their future in the promised land. Moses plainly explained the covenant God gave to Israel at Mount Sinai but with a new focus applicable to the current generation and the generations that would be raised in Canaan. He called the Israelites to obedience so God's purposes would be accomplished in and through the nation in their new land — for their good and God's glory. Finally, Moses transferred leadership to Joshua.

Let's get started digging into these *themes of Deuteronomy* to understand more deeply how God's work with the Israelites *transfers into our lives today.*

MAJOR MOMENTS
in *Deuteronomy*

Week *One*

DEUTERONOMY 1:1-18	Moses looked back at the road God's people had traveled.
DEUTERONOMY 1:19-46	The Israelites rejected God's promise.
DEUTERONOMY 2	The nation received a second chance after the discipline of the desert.
DEUTERONOMY 3	Moses and the Israelites acted in obedience.
DEUTERONOMY 4	Yahweh spoke to the Israelites out of the midst of the fire at Mount Sinai.

Week *Two*

DEUTERONOMY 5	Yahweh, the covenant God, spoke to His people.
DEUTERONOMY 6	Moses reminded Israel of the foundational commandment.
DEUTERONOMY 7	God chose Israel for His purposes.
DEUTERONOMY 8	Moses warned Israel not to forget the Lord after their success.
DEUTERONOMY 9	Moses urged the Israelites to see themselves as God saw them.

Week *Three*

DEUTERONOMY 10	Relationship with God was the foundation of the covenant.
DEUTERONOMY 11	Living in a covenant relationship presented a choice every day.
DEUTERONOMY 12-13	Moses explained acceptable worship and condemned idolatry.
DEUTERONOMY 14	Moses reviewed dietary and tithing commands.
DEUTERONOMY 15	Radical generosity reflected the God of radical blessing.

Week *Four*

DEUTERONOMY 16:1-20	Moses gave instructions for three feasts ordained by God so Israel would remember His provision.
DEUTERONOMY 16:21-17:20	Moses condemned idolatry and gave guidance for Israel's future kings.
DEUTERONOMY 18	The Lord provided for Levi's descendants, forbade pagan practices and spoke of another prophet.
DEUTERONOMY 19	Moses spoke of God's laws for cities of refuge and fair settlement of disputes.
DEUTERONOMY 20	Moses explained God's laws of warfare for Israel.

Week *Five*

DEUTERONOMY 21	Moses addressed situations relating to several of the Ten Commandments.
DEUTERONOMY 22	Details of various laws, including laws about sexual purity, were explained.
DEUTERONOMY 23	Moses addressed laws regarding the assembly of the Lord, among other commands.
DEUTERONOMY 24-25	Laws were given to protect the poor and needy of Israel, and God told Israel to remember and destroy Amalek.
DEUTERONOMY 26	Moses commanded Israel to give their best to the Lord and obey Him with all their hearts and souls.

Week *Six*

DEUTERONOMY 27	Moses commanded Israel to remember God, and the covenant curses were revealed.
DEUTERONOMY 28:1-14	Moses explained the covenant blessings for obedience.
DEUTERONOMY 28:15-68	More covenant curses for disobedience were given.
DEUTERONOMY 29	God renewed His covenant just before Israel entered the promised land.
DEUTERONOMY 30	Moses prophesied Israel's rebellion and repentance and God's restoration.

Week *Seven*

DEUTERONOMY 31:1-13	Moses encouraged Israel and Joshua.
DEUTERONOMY 31:14-29	Joshua was commissioned, and Israel's future was prophesied.
DEUTERONOMY 31:30-32:52	God gave Moses a song of remembrance for Israel.
DEUTERONOMY 33	Moses called the tribes of Israel together to bless them.
DEUTERONOMY 34	After meeting God at the top of Mount Nebo, Moses died.

Week One

Day 1

Moses began his words to Israel with a look back at the past. As the nation approached their promised land, we remember the Israelites had been here before, just 13 months after God delivered them from Egypt. (Numbers 10:11) (For a reminder, review the Israelites' backstory on pages 4-6.)

But because that first generation refused to believe God could fulfill His promise, the whole nation turned around and headed back into the desert for 38 more long years.

Moses stated in Deuteronomy 1:2 that the journey from Mount Sinai (also called Horeb) to the plains of Moab could have taken just 11 days! Talk about a delay!

According to Deuteronomy 1:8b, God had said,

"GO IN AND _____

_____ OF THE LAND ..."

In contrast, what had the Israelite spies said in Numbers 13:31?

Some translations of Numbers 13:31 use the words *"We can't."* Just like the Israelites, we sometimes say "I can't do this" when God has set a task before us that requires faith in His power rather than reliance on our own ability.

Reflect on a time in your past when you told God "I can't" and then experienced a delay in reaching a destination you had hoped to reach sooner. What did you learn from this experience?

As we move past our past, let's ask God to forgive us for the times we have expressed the unbelief of "I can't," and instead let's offer the response of faith that says, "I can't, but You can." Let's focus on God's power rather than our fears.

What if we aren't sure if God will fulfill His purposes in our lives? One of the best ways to increase our faith is to get to know who God is. As we learn about God's character, our knowledge of Him increases, and so will our faith. (Hebrews 11:6)

Let's explore God's faithfulness in the passages below. Read each verse and write the main idea in your own words. (See Genesis 15:18 as an example.)

GOD'S PROMISE	GOD'S ACTIONS
GENESIS 15:18 God promised land to Abraham's descendants	DEUTERONOMY 1:8
GENESIS 22:17	DEUTERONOMY 1:10
GENESIS 22:18	ACTS 13:23
1 JOHN 2:25; JOHN 6:40	JOHN 3:16

God is always faithful to His promises and to His purposes. It does not depend on us! (2 Timothy 2:13)

Write out Hebrews 10:23 below.

Let's reflect on the truth that God is faithful to forgive us when we ask Him and let's thank Him that He remains faithful in spite of our past sin.

Day 2

In today's reading, Moses continued to recall the details of the Israelites' rebellion from 38 years ago, when God had swiftly brought His people through the wilderness to their promised land.

After sending spies to explore the territory, what fact did all the spies agree on? (Deuteronomy 1:25)

Compare verses 28 and 32-33 of Numbers 13 with Moses' retelling in Deuteronomy 1:28. Circle each time these verses say *"we saw"* or *"we have seen."* What did the spies see in the land that caused the people to fear?

This first generation had also *seen* God's miraculous power over Egypt through the plagues, and they had *seen* their firstborn sons spared in the Passover; they had *seen* their enemies destroyed in the Red Sea. Yet those same Israelites stood at the brink of the land where God had led them and did not believe He could fulfill His promise to bring them in. (Deuteronomy 1:32)

Just like the Israelites, we sometimes get tripped up by what we see even when God has instructed us to follow Him in faith. We often choose to walk by sight rather than obey His Word.

Reflect on a time you chose not to obey God because circumstances seemed fearful in your eyes. What were the results of your choice?

How can you make a different choice to walk in faith next time you feel afraid?

As we put our past behind us, we can ask God to help us offer the response of faith that says, "In spite of what I see, I will believe what You said." We can live with purpose as we focus on God's protection and power rather than our own limited vision. We can move forward with eyes of faith. (1 John 4:4)

Unbelief didn't just keep Israel out of the promised land; those who had rejected Yahweh's promise received the just consequences of their rebellion.

According to Deuteronomy 1:34-35, what were the consequences for those who would not believe?

God always acts in justice toward sin, but in His mercy, He rarely acts instantly because He is slow to anger. (Numbers 14:18; Psalm 145:8) God's justice can look frightening, but we understand His justice always works in cooperation with His mercy.

The sacrifice of Jesus demonstrates this beautiful balance. Like the Israelites', our unbelief will bring consequences. But praise God that, through Jesus Christ, He offers us redemption from every failure.

Write what you learn about God's justice from each of these verses.

PSALM 33:5

PSALM 9:7-8

DEUTERONOMY 10:18

DEUTERONOMY 32:4

Write out Isaiah 30:18 in the space below, and thank God for His righteousness, justice and steadfast love.

Day 3

The nation received a second chance after the discipline of the desert.

In recounting the disobedience of the Israelites, Moses had pointed out their lack of faith in Yahweh and reminded them their years of wandering could have been avoided. But he was still not finished looking back. While it had to be difficult for the Israelites to hear Moses recount their sin, the lessons to be learned were of critical importance.

Read Deuteronomy 2:1. How did Moses describe the 38 years of wandering in the wilderness?

Moses did not pause here in his address to talk about the difficulty of those many years of wandering; rather, he pointed out God's actions and words to Israel in the wilderness.

How did God treat them during those wandering years? (Deuteronomy 2:7)

What does this communicate about God's love for His people and His desire to give them a second chance?

Finally, after all those of the rebellious generation had passed away, the time arrived for God to turn the Israelites around, and He pointed them north toward the promised land once again. Moses now mentioned three nations the Israelites cautiously passed by on their journey. God was firm that those nations were not to be engaged in battle.

Who were those nations?

1. DEUTERONOMY 2:4: The descendants of _____, who lived in Seir.

2. DETERONOMY 2:9: The descendants of _____, called the nation of Moab, from the land of Ar.

3. DEUTERONOMY 2:19: Also the descendants of _____, the people of Ammon.

Not only did Moses remind Israel they had failed to enter their own promised land, but he brought up their distant relatives who had obeyed God and entered the land He had given to them. The descendants of Esau and Lot (relatives of the Jewish patriarchs Jacob and Abraham) hadn't backed down from taking the land God offered them. They actually overcame some very familiar problems.

Read Deuteronomy 2:10 and 2:21. How are the conquered people described?

Who destroyed these enemies of the descendants of Lot and Esau? (v. 21)

Yahweh is sovereign not only over His own people but over all nations, rulers and peoples.

It is never easy to hear someone tell us what we have done wrong. But often the reality is we cannot move past our past until we recognize our need to change direction. Thank God for the example of others who have obeyed Him. When we confess our rebellious attitudes, we are finally able to move toward a new beginning.

WHAT DOES IT MEAN THAT GOD IS SOVEREIGN?
• God made all things; therefore, He is the ruler with supreme authority and absolute power over all things. (Colossians 1:17; 1 Peter 5:11)
• God is neither the work of our hands nor a god of our imagination. (Acts 17:25)
• God has the authority (right), power and wisdom to do all that He pleases. (Romans 9:15, 19-21)
• Every part of God's creation is under His will and rule. (Revelation 4:11)
• Every event and situation is under His rule. (Psalm 103:19; Job 42:2)

Still "flashing back" to Israel's past, Deuteronomy 3 retells a story of obedience. After the defeat of Sihon, (Deuteronomy 2:26-37) the Israelites experienced the opportunity to demonstrate their faith in God's words a second time. Og, the king of Bashan, came out against them in battle.

After so much focus on the Israelites' history of rebellion and disobedience, let's rejoice in their willingness to obey God in these two battles. Let's celebrate as Moses reminds us of their choice not to walk in the rebellion of their fathers. Today, let's focus on a characteristic this generation of Israelites finally demonstrated, a characteristic that should be noticeable in God's covenant people in any generation — obedience.

How many cities did the king of Bashan control? (Deuteronomy 3:4)

What fortifications did these cities have? (v. 5)

In obedience, the Israelites moved out into battle, **even though their enemy was strong.**

Which 2 1/2 tribes received the lands of Sihon and Og as their inheritance, east of the Jordan River? (vv. 12-13)

What act of sacrifice did Moses ask of these tribes? What did the men have to do before inhabiting the land with their families? (vv. 18-20)

In obedience, these tribes chose to fight with their fellow countrymen, **even though it was a sacrifice.**

Similarly, Moses struggled greatly with God's instruction that he would not enter the promised land with the Israelites, which would be a great sacrifice.

Describe his prayer as he asked God to reconsider. (vv. 23-25) Have you ever prayed a prayer like this one?

In obedience, Moses accepted God's choice, **even though he was grieved and did not completely understand**.

Reflect on a time you resisted obedience because you weren't sure you would succeed … or because it was just too great a sacrifice to make … or because God had not acted as you expected …

Oh, there are so many reasons we might use as rationalizations to disobey, but we, like the Israelites, will benefit when we obey God by faith. We do not see all He has planned, but we know, even when obedience seems challenging, He has a purpose. Even when obedience seems inconvenient, He has a purpose. Even when obedience seems disappointing, He has a purpose.

As we move past our past, may we seek to obey God's Word, walk in His strength and yield to His purposes rather than our own.

KNOW THEREFORE
TODAY, AND *lay it
to your heart*, THAT
THE LORD IS GOD
IN HEAVEN ABOVE
AND ON THE
EARTH BENEATH;
there is no other.

DEUTERONOMY 4:39

Day 5

DEUTERONOMY 4

Yahweh spoke to the Israelites out of the midst of the fire at Mount Sinai.

As Moses wrapped up his first address, he challenged the Israelites to listen and do ...
They were to listen to what? (Deuteronomy 4:1)

They were to do what? (v. 5)

What kind of nation would Israel become if they would keep and follow God's statutes?

DEUTERONOMY 4:6 -

DEUTERONOMY 4:7 -

DEUTERONOMY 4:8 -

From what other sources would the Israelites and their children be tempted to seek these benefits in the years to come? (vv. 16-19)

Moses didn't just present to the Israelites the benefits of following God; he also warned them about the dangers of idolatry they would face in the promised land.

What characteristic of God is mentioned in verse 24?

It's right for God to be jealous for what is His. God's love for His people is perfect. Only He, Yahweh, had delivered His people. Only He guarded and cared for them. God jealously insisted that His people never follow after other gods, which would lead them astray and bring them harm.[1]

No other god offered His words of wisdom and understanding. No other god was living, so no other god could be present with the people and meet their needs. No other god provided righteousness to His people. Only Yahweh was — and is — to be worshiped.

How have you been tempted to seek wisdom or solutions to life's difficulties from other sources rather than God?

Since God freely gives wisdom, His presence and righteousness, how might seeking these things from other sources be comparable to worshiping an idol?

God offered Israel His wisdom, presence and righteousness through the covenant of the law. (Deuteronomy 4:6-8) Today, God offers us the same — and more — through the new covenant. He offers us His wisdom and understanding in His precious Word, not only the statutes and rules in the Old Testament but the example of their perfect fulfillment in Jesus, found in the New Testament. (Psalm 19:7-11; Matthew 5:17) He offers us His presence, dwelling within us in the Person of His Holy Spirit. (Ephesians 1:13) And He offers us peace through His own righteousness, purchased by the death and resurrection of Jesus. (2 Corinthians 5:21)

We all have tried to satisfy our own needs through work, relationships, possessions or any other idol we have put above Him. Instead, let's claim the righteousness of Jesus as our own by faith. Let's welcome the presence of the Holy Spirit and seek the wisdom of His Word so we can live with purpose today.

Weekend *Reflection*

This week we took a seat on the grass with the Israelites and listened as Moses presented his first farewell message. Moses had walked a long time with the Israelites, and he began by remembering their past. It was important for Israel to confront their history of sin and rebellion. If they wanted to reposition themselves to receive God's blessing, they needed to assess their wrong turns honestly.

The first generation of Israelites said "we can't" to Yahweh. They chose to ignore the faithfulness God had demonstrated, again and again, to His promises. They would not believe God's words of promise to them. They would not walk by faith in God's mighty power. Their rebellion brought just consequences.

Later, the next generation of Israelites demonstrated obedience even though it was challenging and inconvenient. Moses obeyed God, too, even though the consequences of his sin were disappointing for him.

Only by placing their faith firmly in what God had done for them and in the promises He had made to them would the Israelites have the strength and courage to move forward into their future. Admitting the mistakes of the past was the first important step in reaching God's promised blessing, and it's the same for us today.

PRAYER:

Thank You, God, for forgiving me when I confess the sin and rebellion of my past. Thank You that You do not treat me as my sins deserve. Thank You for causing me to walk in Your ways with increasing consistency every day.

Lord, I pray Your words today from Psalm 103:10-14:

"He does not deal with us according to our sins,
nor repay us according to our iniquities.
For as high as the heavens are above the earth,
so great is his steadfast love toward those who fear him;
as far as the east is from the west,
so far does he remove our transgressions from us.
As a father shows compassion to his children,
so the LORD shows compassion to those who fear him.
For he knows our frame;
he remembers that we are dust."

In Jesus' name, amen.

Notes

Notes

Week
Two

Day 6

DEUTERONOMY 5
Yahweh, the covenant God, spoke to His people.

Moses began his second message to the Israelites with emphasis on the overarching principles of the covenant established between God and the Israelites at Horeb (Mount Sinai). We call these covenant principles the Decalogue, or the Ten Words, or most commonly the Ten Commandments.

Previously, in Exodus 20:1, *"God spoke all these words."* Later, in Deuteronomy, many scholars believe Moses simply recited the Ten Words, as a pastor might read a passage of Scripture before beginning his message in a worship service.[1] Moses then proceeded to elaborate on the application of the Ten Words all the way through Deuteronomy.

These Ten Words represent a universal and permanent way of life for the people of God.

In Deuteronomy 5:5, Moses declared these commands of the covenant to be the word of whom?

The fact that God spoke directly to His people is an amazing reality! Other nations had no such communication with their gods.

Read the following passages, and comment on what the Israelites saw and heard:

EXODUS 19:16-19 -

DEUTERONOMY 4:10-13 -

DEUTERONOMY 5:22-24 -

The Israelites were overwhelmed by the presence of God in their midst.

What did they ask of Moses in Exodus 20:19?

God accepted the Israelites' fear and awe and allowed Moses to act as their mediator, teaching them all God's words.[2] Later, Jesus came as the greater Teacher, and He expanded the people's understanding of God's ways even further as He walked among them.

How is Jesus described in John 1:1, John 1:14 and Revelation 19:13?

Read John 17:8. What did Jesus speak to His people?

Jesus continued God's communication with humanity. He was (and is) the exact image of God, speaking the word of God. (Hebrews 1:1-3)

Write out Luke 11:28.

Describe a time you heard but refused to act on the Truth of God revealed to you in His Word. How can you move forward now to be a "hearer" and "keeper" of the Word?

Just as the Israelites received the Word of God revealed directly to them, we can open our Bibles, the Word of God revealed to us, and ask the Holy Spirit for His power to daily obey and follow God. We can also ask God to forgive us for the times we have disregarded the example He has given us in His Son, and He is faithful to forgive us when we ask. (1 John 1:9) In this way, we can live with purpose and bring glory to our living, communicating God.

True love of God is not only spoken but lived. So it was Moses' desire to encourage the Israelites, beyond just understanding the covenant, to live out the covenant. Moses wished to motivate the people to obey God's commands.

What benefits of obedience did he mention in Deuteronomy 6:3?

Beginning in verse 4, we find a passage that the Jews refer to as the Shema. The word *Shema* is translated "to listen" in English, but it means so much more. In the Hebrew language, *shema* incorporated hearing, understanding *and* responding.[1] So when Moses said "hear" (or "listen") he was demanding action, not just acknowledgment.

Write out Deuteronomy 6:4-5 in the space below.

The Shema communicates that Yahweh is the only God. In this truth, we find the basis upon which all God's other commandments stand.

What instruction does Jesus give in Mark 12:29-30?

God's love *toward* His people is always represented by action. So the response God seeks *from* His people is also one of action. This is not a love of wavering emotion or fickle attention.

God seeks the loving response of obedience,
offered willingly to the Deliverer, from those freed from the bondage of slavery.
God seeks the loving response of gratitude,
given in wholehearted devotion to the Provider, from those who had nothing of their own.
God seeks the loving response of loyalty,
presented joyfully to the Sovereign, from those who have no greater desire than to serve the Master they love.

Below, write a prayer asking that you will understand more deeply how to give *"all your heart,"* *"all your soul"* and *"all your might"* to God (Deuteronomy 6:5).

In the reality of life in their new land, the Israelites would be confronted with two paths away from God: to bow to no one (God included) because they walked in their own strength and righteousness, or to bow to other gods. Both would bring disaster.

In the reality of our lives, we, too, are often tempted to walk in our own strength or to worship other people or activities, seeking satisfaction apart from God.

Which of these two alternatives do you find most common in your life?

To move past our past, we will need to confess our desire to serve God *alongside* other objects of worship, including ourselves, and we will need to ask His forgiveness. We can only live with purpose as we diligently listen and act, offering to Him alone all that we are. He is the only One worthy of our worship. Yahweh is God alone!

Ten Words

Read each of the "Ten Words" from Exodus and from Deuteronomy, and summarize the commands in the chart below.

EXODUS	DEUTERONOMY	SUMMARY OF THE COMMANDMENT
EXODUS 20:2-3	DEUTERONOMY 5:6-7	
EXODUS 20:4-6	DEUTERONOMY 5:8-10	
EXODUS 20:7	DEUTERONOMY 5:11	
EXODUS 20:8-11	DEUTERONOMY 5:12-15	

EXODUS	DEUTERONOMY	SUMMARY OF THE COMMANDMENT
EXODUS 20:12	DEUTERONOMY 5:16	
EXODUS 20:13	DEUTERONOMY 5:17	
EXODUS 20:14	DEUTERONOMY 5:18	
EXODUS 20:15	DEUTERONOMY 5:19	
EXODUS 20:16	DEUTERONOMY 5:20	
EXODUS 20:17	DEUTERONOMY 5:21	

Day 8

God chose Israel as His own special people, His own treasured possession. Shortly after the Israelites were delivered from Egypt, when they arrived at Mount Sinai (Horeb), God gave Moses this promise in Exodus 19:5-6.

What does God call Israel in Exodus 19:6?

What additional descriptions of the Israelites do you find in Deuteronomy 7:6?

According to Deuteronomy 7:7-8, why did God choose the Israelites?

Describe a time you were chosen for an assignment. Were you willing? Did you feel prepared? Did you have the strength required, or did you need help?

This assignment brought great responsibilities for the nation of Israel. The land God had promised them was occupied by nations that lived in sin and rebellion against God. Although these nations had knowledge of God's power and had seen His acts on behalf of Israel, they had disregarded all opportunities to repent. The time determined for God's just judgment had arrived, and Israel would be the instrument God used for His purpose. (Deuteronomy 7:9-10; Deuteronomy 7:23-24)

What did God direct regarding the nations that were conquered? (vv. 2-3)

What additional requirements did God give that had to do with the places of idol worship in the conquered land? (vv. 5, 25)

We have been chosen for God's purposes in our generation, just as the Israelites were.

Read 1 Peter 2:9-10. Who are we as God's people?

What have we been called to do as God's people?

Have we been called as God's people by our own merits? Can you provide a scripture that supports your answer?

Remembering this wonderful correlation to God's people in every age, we can confidently engage the enemy in daily struggles against sin and temptation when we live in reliance on God's power over our past, (Romans 8:1-3; Ephesians 2:1-5) God's power in our present (1 John 4:4; Romans 8:4) and God's power to secure our future. (Romans 8:31-32; Romans 8:37)

We've talked a lot about Israel's past so far in our study of Deuteronomy. In today's passage, Moses talked about their future as he strongly cautioned God's people against forgetting Yahweh, which would lead to grave consequences when they ceased to walk in obedience to His commands.

What two ways did Moses explain the Israelites might forget God in the promised land?

DEUTERONOMY 8:14: *"then your _____ _____ _____ _____,* *and you forget the Lord your God ..."*

DEUTERONOMY 8:19: *"And if you forget the Lord your God and _____ _____* *_____ _____ ..."*

Two actions that would cause God's people to forget Him were pride and idolatry. Of these two, Moses first cautioned the Israelites against having hearts *"lifted up"* against God in pride or arrogance, and Moses focused on pride in Deuteronomy 8.

Moses reminded the Israelites that God had a purpose for the years of wilderness wandering. What was that purpose? (Deuteronomy 8:3)

Moses recognized the wilderness period was a test for the Israelites. Those who stood now listening to Moses had humbled themselves to follow Yahweh in faith, thankful for His provision and protection rather than grumbling and complaining against Him as their fathers had done.

The fact that they were ready and waiting to enter the promised land was proof their faith and obedience had grown in the wilderness. But Moses advised them to prepare, for other tests would come.

Moses cautioned that the challenges they would encounter after settling in the promised land would be very different from the challenges of the wilderness. In the desert, they had learned to rely on God in their lack, in their need. In the promised land, they would need to rely on God in abundance. In their prosperity, Moses warned, they would face the temptation to forget Yahweh.[1]

What would the Israelites experience in the promised land? (Deuteronomy 8:7-9)

Moses forewarned them against what response? (v. 17)

Reflect on a time you were tempted to attribute your success to your own abilities or efforts. How can you remember God in your success today?

Self-sufficiency is an illusion. Just like the Israelites, we must be intentional in our response to honor Yahweh in our prosperity.

Just like the Israelites, we must "_____ _____ *lest [we] forget the* LORD *[our] God ...*" (v. 11).

Whether we are in a wilderness or in abundance, only proper dependence on God will keep us from the hardhearted rebellion that forgets, or ignores, His hand of protection and provision in our every day.

Write out Deuteronomy 8:10 as a reminder to bless God today and every day.

Day 10

Moses urged the Israelites to see themselves as God saw them.

It seems our Israelites are a stubborn bunch. Moses addressed their attitude of pride in yesterday's lesson, and in today's reading Moses cautioned again about a wrong attitude of the heart.

What might an Israelite have been tempted to give as the reason God's enemies had been defeated? (Deuteronomy 9:4)

For what two reasons were the nations really driven out before the Israelites? (v. 5)

Rather than a righteous group, how did Moses describe the Israelites?

DEUTERONOMY 9:6-7

DEUTERONOMY 9:8

DEUTERONOMY 9:12-13

Moses reviewed the sad story of the golden calf in detail, and he mentioned three other examples of rebellion: Taberah, Massah, and Kibroth-hattaavah. Let's look more closely.

TABERAH

Read Numbers 11:1-3. Describe the Israelites' attitude at Taberah.

How did God demonstrate mercy and/or judgment?

MASSAH

Read Exodus 17:1-7. Describe the Israelites' attitude in verses 1-3.

How did God demonstrate mercy and/or judgment?

KIBROTH-HATTAAVAH

Read Numbers 11:4-34. Describe the Israelites' attitude in verses 4-6.

How did God demonstrate mercy and/or judgment? (By the way, Kibroth-hattaavah means "graves of craving.")

Our covenant God is slow to anger. Even His judgment is tempered by His steadfast love and mercy.

Write out Psalm 86:15 below.

God remained faithful to His covenant people, even in His anger, displeasure and grief over their persistent sin, even when Israel provoked Him again and again and again. God's judgment came on those Israelites who refused to recognize Yahweh had any authority over them, who continued to walk in self-righteousness and rebellion against the God who made them and delivered them and offered them life. But because God is slow to anger, He always allowed opportunity for repentance before bringing just consequences on the guilty.

God offers forgiveness for our rebellion and sin even though we don't deserve it. Praise God that He is slow to anger in the face of our self-centeredness. We can live with purpose as we remember God hears our prayers of repentance and confession. Because of His mercy, we are redeemed!

Read Lamentations 3:22-23, and thank God that His mercy is new every morning.

Weekend *Reflection*

This week, we learned Yahweh is a God who communicates. He spoke His Truth directly to His people at Mount Sinai and through Moses to the next generation. Today, God speaks to us through His Son, His Spirit and His Word. (Hebrews 1:1-2; John 16:13; 2 Timothy 3:16)

One purpose of God's communication in Numbers was to provide instructions for action. The Ten Commandments represented the principles of that revelation. Moses understood that hearing without doing wasn't *listening* — in fact, it actually constitutes rebellion to hear but choose not to do what God directs. (Luke 6:46)

God chose Israel because He had some tasks for them to accomplish. As God worked out His purposes through them, they would learn to walk in the obedience of faith. Their chosen status was not because they were better than other nations; in fact, God promised that if His people walked in the same sins as other nations, they would also walk in the same judgment.

The Israelites would be tempted, in their abundance, to lift up their hearts in pride and forget God. Only by acting on God's words would they gain the blessings promised for their future.

PRAYER:

Thank You, God, for choosing me although I am unworthy. Thank You that you give me Your law, that I may meditate on and learn Your ways. Help me to act in obedience to Your Word so I may participate in Your present purposes in this world.

Lord, I pray Your words today from Psalm 1:1-3:

"Blessed is the man
who walks not in the counsel of the wicked,
nor stands in the way of sinners,
nor sits in the seat of scoffers;
but his delight is in the law of the LORD,
and on his law he meditates day and night.

He is like a tree
planted by streams of water
that yields its fruit in its season,
and its leaf does not wither.
In all that he does, he prospers."

In Jesus' name, amen.

Notes

Notes

Week Three

In Deuteronomy 9, Moses presented examples of Israel's rebellious track record. In Deuteronomy 10, he continued the story of God's mercy at Mount Sinai after the Israelites' idolatry. In his review, Moses skipped past some of the details of his intercession on behalf of the Israelites, so let's look back ...

Read Exodus 32:30-35.

What amazing request did Moses make on behalf of God's people? (Exodus 32:32)

Moses confessed the sin and failure of the people. Knowing the Israelites had fallen from God's ways, he offered himself in their place and was even willing to take their punishment. Moses prayed for God's presence to remain with them. In response to Moses' humility, God proclaimed His mercy, love and forgiveness to those who did not deserve it. God remained faithful to His promises, in spite of His people's sin.

God brought Moses back up on the mountain, where He rewrote His Ten Words on a second set of tablets, replacing those Moses had smashed. (Deuteronomy 10:1-2)

Reassured that God's presence would go with them, (Exodus 33:14) the Israelites moved forward on their journey. (Deuteronomy 10:6-7) The faithfulness of God was the foundation on which this covenant relationship stood.

What does "faithfulness" mean to you? Is faithfulness expected of both people in a relationship?

In Deuteronomy 10:12, Moses called God's people to remember the faithfulness they were to offer back to God, asking:

"WHAT DOES THE LORD YOUR GOD

_____ _____ _____ "?

Since Moses asked and answered, write out his five instructions. (vv. 12-13)

What Does the Lord *Your God* Require of You?

DEUTERONOMY 10:12-13

We "fear the Lord" by recognizing His greatness and power, by acknowledging His mighty and awesome deeds in the heavens and the earth.

Meditate on Deuteronomy 10:14 and 10:17a.

We "walk in all His ways" in part by interacting justly and compassionately in our communities.

Meditate on Deuteronomy 10:18-19 and Psalm 146:5-10.

We "love Him" by responding to the knowledge that He reached out first and chose us in love.

Meditate on Deuteronomy 10:15 and 1 John 4:19.

We "serve the Lord" with all our heart and all our soul by submitting humbly to His will.

Meditate on Deuteronomy 10:16 and Ezekiel 36:26.

We "keep the commandments" by knowing and obeying the Word of God. We begin by studying and valuing the Truth He has given us.

Meditate on Deuteronomy 10:4 and 2 Timothy 2:15.

Active relationship is the heart of the covenant. God chose the Israelites so they might walk in partnership with Him. He has chosen us in Christ Jesus for the same. Moses challenged the Israelites to respond rightly. May we respond rightly, as well.

Day 12

DEUTERONOMY 11

Living in a covenant relationship presented a choice every day.

In today's reading, Moses continued to recount Yahweh's amazing deeds, encouraging God's people to consider all the many ways they had seen their God in action.

Like the Israelites, we are prone to forget God is powerful in our todays, not just in our yesterdays. Moses used the word "today" seven times in Deuteronomy 11 as he spoke of a perpetual "today" of abundance and blessing for God's covenant people if they chose to obey Him.

What do you notice about available water in these descriptions?

DEUTERONOMY 8:7 *(a verse from a previous chapter)* -

DEUTERONOMY 11:11 *(a verse from today's chapter)* -

Was water readily available in the same way for the Israelites in Egypt? (Deuteronomy 11:10)

What was the Israelites' experience with water in the wilderness? (Exodus 15:22; Exodus 17:1)

In the wilderness, there had often been no natural drinking water. God's people cried out to Him because He is the source of all water.

In Egypt, God's people didn't look to the sky but to the Nile River as their source of water, which could be obtained through their own efforts using irrigation canals and ditches. They had to work for their water, and it was a limited resource.

Read Deuteronomy 11:14-15. Note the words *"he will give."* In the promised land, if they obeyed, God would be their only source. They would live in the blessing of covenant relationship with their God, or if they disobeyed, they would live under the curse of their own effort and striving.

After many, many years of their rebellious living, the prophet Jeremiah condemned the nation. How did God's words, spoken by Jeremiah, describe the Israelites' evil in Jeremiah 2:12-13? (Note: A cistern in ancient times was a cylindrical hole dug 3-10 meters below ground to gather rainwater.)

Reflect on a time when you, like the Israelites, rejected the true Source of life and blessing, the true Source of living water, in your life. Did you attempt to dig your own cistern, hoping to find the water your soul needed? Did you find the cistern able to provide living water?

Jesus came to a people determined to satisfy their own needs.

What was the great blessing He offered to the broken woman seeking water in John 4:7-14?

Today, as the woman at the well did, we can make a choice to set aside our past, turn away from the cisterns of our own making and admit that only our covenant God can satisfy us with His living water. We can live with purpose today and every day as we cry out to Jesus, knowing *"he will give"* all that we need. He will never turn us away.

The Israelites had lived by a certain pattern in Egypt. Living among a pagan, worldly people for so long, Israel lost sight of who Yahweh was and who they were to be as His people. Immersed in a culture of gods and goddesses, of wrongful worship and veneration, they forgot the personal relationship their fathers — Abraham, Isaac and Jacob — had with the one true God.

How did Yahweh clearly direct His people about idol worship in Deuteronomy 12:4?

But when God delivered His nation from Egypt, the patterns of worship they had known traveled along with them. The golden calf (Exodus 32) represented an attempt to use those patterns to worship Yahweh.

As they traveled the wilderness in isolation for a generation, Yahweh continued to teach them and reprove them, correct them and train them in righteousness. Through Moses, Yahweh presented worship as it should be.

Read 2 Timothy 3:16-17. What does verse 17 give as the reason God works to correct and train His people?

God's laws are His gracious direction for how to live! God shared with His people how to remain true to Him and so live in His blessing. His Ten Words were a basic structure to identify the patterns of life the Israelites needed to submit to His rule.

In Deuteronomy 12 Moses began with the pattern of the people's worship. The Israelites were about to enter a land where they would be dispersed across a large geographical area; through Moses, God gave instructions that the Israelites would travel to a central location for worship.

How is that location described in Deuteronomy 12:5?

make it count

What were the Israelites to bring in worship? (Deuteronomy 12:11; Deuteronomy 12:26)

Following God's pattern for worship continued the pattern of covenant relationship.
    Who came in worship? (vv. 12, 18)

Describe the Israelites' attitudes and actions when they gathered to worship Yahweh. (vv. 7, 18b)

God brought the Israelites out of a land of idols and provided His pattern for their worship of Him; only if they would internalize His pattern would they escape the old patterns of idol worship and living for self.
    From whom did Moses warn that temptation toward their old patterns might come?

DEUTERONOMY 13:1-3 -

DEUTERONOMY 13:6-7 -

DEUTERONOMY 13:12-13 -

We are all tempted to worship God using the patterns most familiar to us, the ones we know in our families, friend groups, cultures or communities. But these patterns may not be aligned with God's ways. Just like the Israelites needed God's words and direction to break, or even recognize, their old patterns, so we need God's Word as a mirror to show us the ways of God, to teach us and train us in His righteousness.

We might easily appreciate the significance of Moses' instructions about right worship in Deuteronomy Chapters 12 and 13, but it's also worth noting that even activities as common as the Israelites' food choices reflected the God they served and set them apart from the Canaanite nations around them.

Moses continually encouraged God's people, in every aspect of the covenant, to respond to Yahweh with more than a required, forced obedience to external laws. He wanted their response to always be one of joyful relationship.

Read Deuteronomy 14:1-2. What words or phrases speak of a relationship?

This is not the first time Moses had referred to Yahweh as Israel's Father.

Read Deuteronomy 1:31 and 8:5. Describe the relationship in these passages.

So what does a relationship have to do with diet? The Israelites were essentially invited to eat at their Father's table, to feast with Him, the King.

In ancient cultures, those whom a king wished to honor were often extended an invitation to eat at his table. This act of a sovereign demonstrated care and compassion to those with lesser resources.

In each of the passages below, note who offered a place at their table, and to whom:

GENESIS 43:33-34

2 SAMUEL 9:6-7

2 KINGS 25:27-29

LUKE 22:28-30

The Israelites looked forward to the feasting and celebrations that would come in the promised land. Who did Moses remind them not to neglect in Deuteronomy 14:27 and 14:29?

The Israelites were to follow God's compassionate example. The blessings of the land came from God. As He bountifully shared with them, they were to share with those who did not have land of their own, like the Levites (Deuteronomy 10:9) or the less fortunate.

Meditate on Deuteronomy 8:18 and reflect on a time you received bountifully from God's hand. Did you share the blessings of God generously? What could you do this week to share the blessings you currently have?

As we move past our past, we can loosen our grip as we realize all we hold in our hands has been given to us by God. We can live with purpose today as we give generously in order to serve others and bring glory to God.

Write out Matthew 25:21 and thank the King for daily opportunities to steward wisely what we hold in our hands.

Day 15

DEUTERONOMY 15

Radical generosity reflected the God of radical blessing.

Living as God's covenant people would change the Israelites. Moses reminded them they had provided nothing for themselves in the many years since Yahweh delivered them from Egypt. They had been the recipients of God's merciful, undeserved kindness. Moses now directed them to mirror the grace and mercy they'd received — by extending generous care to others.

In Deuteronomy 14, Moses began to expound the many ways God's covenant people were to live in generosity, and he expanded that theme in Deuteronomy 15: Those who serve a generous God should walk in generosity themselves.

Read 1 John 4:19. How does this verse fuel generosity?

Our love toward people, our acts of mercy and kindness, must be rooted deeply in the fact that Yahweh loves us.

As God's people gave to others, how did Deuteronomy 15:10 describe what their attitudes should be?

What truth does Moses reference in Deuteronomy 15:15 as the motivation for right covenant attitudes?

What a radical reminder of who owns it all. When we are tempted to hold our hands tightly around what God has given us to steward, may we remember the Source of it all.

Jot down key phrases in which Moses used the word "hand" in Deuteronomy 15.

VERSE 3 -

VERSE 7 -

VERSE 8 -

VERSE 11 -

VERSE 13 -

What promise did Moses give Israel for covenant obedience and generosity? (v. 6)

Read 2 Corinthians 9:6-7. Describe what you learn from these verses about how covenant living extends into our lives today.

As we move past our past, we can ask God to help us notice the needs of others. We can begin to live with purpose today as we allow the Lord to draw our attention, in ever-widening circles, to prayer and action on behalf of others.

Jesus said the greatest commandments were to love God and love others.

Write out Romans 13:10 and meditate on what loving others looks like in your life.

Weekend *Reflection*

As a covenant people, the Israelites were in partnership with the living God, the maker of heaven and earth. The Israelites were to follow God's compassionate example, extending the undeserved mercy of God generously to all people in their nation and shining as a light for all nations. (Isaiah 42:6)

The Israelites suffered when they rejected Yahweh's abundant resources and instead sought to satisfy their needs by their own efforts or through idolatry. Moses encouraged them to be always mindful that Yahweh alone was their Provider, their Defender, their Deliverer. They had not gained any of these blessings by their own strength.

Moses condemned idolatry as a sure way to break covenant with Yahweh, whether worshiping other gods instead of or alongside Yahweh, or attempting to represent the Creator as any created thing. No matter who might encourage it — "prophets," beloved family or the larger group in the next city — God's people were to reject idolatry severely, and while we may not worship carved images today, we, too, are called to turn from anything that has taken the place of God in our hearts in the past or the present.

The Israelites would be tempted, in their prosperity, to slip into old patterns of idolatry or self-sufficiency and forget Yahweh. Only by obeying God's covenant commands would they remain safely in their promised land in the future.

PRAYER:

Thank You, God, for providing everything we need for life and godliness. Thank You for Your Word, which directs us and keeps us in Your presence. Help us to remember that all we have received comes from You and that we are to open our hands to others in love, with You as our example.

Lord, I pray Your words today from 2 Peter 1:3-8:

"His divine power has granted to us all things that pertain to life and godliness, through the knowledge of him who called us to his own glory and excellence, by which he has granted to us his precious and very great promises, so that through them you may become partakers of the divine nature, having escaped from the corruption that is in the world because of sinful desire. For this very reason, make every effort to supplement your faith with virtue, and virtue with knowledge, and knowledge with self-control, and self-control with steadfastness, and steadfastness with godliness, and godliness with brotherly affection, and brotherly affection with love. For if these qualities are yours and are increasing, they keep you from being ineffective or unfruitful in the knowledge of our Lord Jesus Christ."

In Jesus' name, amen.

Notes

Notes

Week
Four

Moses gave instructions for three feasts ordained by God so Israel would remember His provision.

Thinking of a feast elicits images of abundant food and celebrations of memorable events with family and friends. Have you ever thought that God originated feasts? In Deuteronomy 16:1-17, the Lord initiated three feasts to be celebrated once His people entered the promised land. Each feast was unique, but all had a common purpose: to unite God's people in community, worship, remembrance and celebration of their God.

According to Deuteronomy 16:1-2, when and where was Passover to be celebrated?

Why was this event so important in the lives of the Jewish people? (See Exodus 12:23-26.)

As Israel remembered God's mighty act of salvation to free them from the bondage of Egypt, they also foreshadowed God's mighty act of salvation that would come through His Son, Jesus Christ. Jesus was led to the cross as the Jewish people were celebrating Passover, carrying their lambs to the temple to be sacrificed.

In Exodus 12, the lambs' blood on the doorposts of Hebrew homes in Egypt had saved them from death and freed them from bondage; likewise, the blood of Jesus, the Lamb of God, saved us and set us free from the bondage of sin and death. In 1 Corinthians 5:7, Paul called Christ *"our Passover lamb."*

Take a minute to remember all that God did by sending Jesus to be sacrificed as your Passover lamb ... and thank Him.

make it count

How much do you know about baking bread? Leaven in biblical times was equivalent to yeast today. Once the leaven was incorporated into the dough, it would take at least three to seven hours for a loaf of bread dough to rise before baking. There was no time to allow the bread to rise as the Israelites prepared to escape from Egypt.

The Feast of Unleavened Bread (the seven days following the night of Passover [Deuteronomy 16:8]) was to commemorate the haste with which the Israelites left Egypt.

Leaven also symbolized sin and corruption; therefore, removing the leaven signified what?

The Feast of Weeks and the Feast of Booths (Deuteronomy 16:9-17) celebrated God's provision for the spring and fall harvests, respectively. The Feast of Booths was also to remind God's people of His faithful provision during their 40 years in the wilderness.

According to Leviticus 23:42-43, why was this feast called the Feast of Booths?

Israel's past was riddled with failures and unfaithfulness, yet God was faithful to keep all His promises and bring them to this new land. He wanted them to remember His mighty works, be thankful for His provision and look forward with courage.

Write a prayer placing your past under the umbrella of God's faithfulness and entrusting Him with your future.

Day 17

Moses condemned idolatry and gave guidance for Israel's future kings.

God had established a covenant with Israel in the wilderness, saying, *"I will walk among you and will be your God, and you shall be my people"* (Leviticus 26:12). Israel was to worship differently, sacrifice differently and behave differently from their neighbors. While other people created the gods they worshiped, the people of Israel worshiped the God of creation, who chose them to be His own people.

Let's revisit Exodus 20:3-4. What were the first two of the Ten Commandments?

1)

2)

According to Deuteronomy 17:2-3, describe what it meant to transgress God's covenant commands about idolatry.

Idolatry was an affront to God and was punishable by stoning. This extreme punishment would be carried out with justice — not only were multiple witnesses required to convict, but they would also throw the first stones of execution. (vv. 5-7)

Verses 7 and 13 of Deuteronomy 17 record two purposes accomplished by executing an idolator. What were those purposes? How do these verses show God's desire to help Israel move past their sins?

Verses 14-20 pivot to a time in the future when Israel would have earthly kings. Knowing that Israel would desire to have kings similar to other nations' once settled in the promised land, God gave specific directives. First and foremost, Israel's kings would be appointed by God.

Three prohibitions were given for Israel's kings. (vv. 16-17) The king must NOT *"acquire"* the following things in excess:

1) _____: that he might not trust in outward power and cease depending on God.

2) _____: that his heart might not be turned to idolatry and forget God.

3) _____: that he might not trust in wealth rather than trusting in God.

God also gave three requirements for Israel's kings to follow.

1) *"... he shall write for himself in a book a _____ _____ _____ _____ ..."* (v. 18)

2) *"And it shall _____ _____ _____..."* (v. 19)

3) *"... and he shall read in it _____ _____ _____ of his life ..."* (v. 19)

Kings of Israel would only be able to rule and lead well by humbly following God's commands. The kings who knew God's law would know God.

How are these commands for Israel's kings still relevant to our lives today? (See verse 20.)

Day 18

The Lord provided for Levi's descendants, forbade pagan practices and spoke of another prophet.

Chosen: a word wrapped with meaning not only in the Old Testament but also today. Israel was chosen by God to be His people, and the descendants of Levi (specifically, descendants of the Levite Aaron) were chosen to be priests. The tribe of Levi may have felt excluded as all the other tribes were given land; however, God had not forgotten them. He gave them the best inheritance of all the tribes. Moses spoke God's words concerning Levi's descendants: *"The Lord is their inheritance"* (Deuteronomy 18:2).

Among other things, this meant the Lord would provide for all their needs. According to verses 1-4, notice the priests would have the *"firstfruits"* of the grains, wine and oil; a portion of the sacrificed animals would be their food, and the first shearling of the sheep meant warm clothing. They would have the finest of all of Israel.

Compare Deuteronomy 18:5 to 1 Peter 2:9 (which you might remember from Day 8 of our study). How are believers today similar to the priestly tribe of Levi?

In verses 9-14, Moses shifted his focus to the heart of the nation of Israel. He made a clear dichotomy between how the nation of Israel was to worship in contrast to their neighbors.

What were some of other nations' practices that Moses specifically noted as detestable to the Lord?

In contrast to following the idolatry and witchcraft of other nations, God's people were to *"be*

_____ *before the Lord your God"* (v. 13).

make it count

According to verses 15-22, to whom were God's people to listen, and to whom were they not to listen?

Not even Joshua, who led God's people after Moses, was truly like Moses, who acted as a special mediator between the people and God; so most scholars agree verse 15 points directly to Jesus Christ. This prophecy was confirmed at Jesus' baptism when the people heard a voice from the cloud say, *"This is my beloved Son, with whom I am well pleased; <u>listen to him</u>"* (Matthew 17:5, emphasis added).

Note that in Deuteronomy 18, God appointed two categories of people to be His servants:
1) Priests: Those who represented the people to God. (Deuteronomy 18:1-8)
2) Prophets: Those who represented God to the people. (Deuteronomy 18:15-22)

According to Hebrews 4:14 and John 6:14, how was Jesus the perfect and ultimate fulfillment of both of those roles?

Read Hebrews 4:15-16 and Hebrews 1:1-3. How does Jesus personally minister to us as a priest and prophet?

Day 19

Moses spoke God's laws for cities of refuge and fair settlement of disputes.

When God spoke the Ten Words from the fire and thunder at Mount Sinai, they were not suggestions but *"commandments"* (Exodus 20:6). He intended them to be the foundation for life for His people. After that day, God gave further explanations and even examples of ways to implement His commandments in everyday living. Through Moses, God addressed broken human relationships in Deuteronomy 19.

What was the Lord's provision for someone who accidentally killed another person? (Deuteronomy 19:1-7)

God's sense of compassion and mercy is revealed in the provision of cities of refuge for those who killed someone unintentionally. These people were allowed to put their mistakes behind them and live faithfully in a new place, giving them a fresh start.

Compare this provision to God's command for a person who intentionally killed someone. (vv. 11-13) What was the difference between the two "manslayers" in God's eyes?

Next, God addressed the sin of covetousness by telling the people they should be content with their boundaries.

Compare Deuteronomy 19:14 to the 10th of the Ten Commandments, in Exodus 20:17.

make it count

Deuteronomy 19:15-20 explained rules for specific situations between two people in conflict. Which phrases give you insight into God's sense of justice and fairness?

Israel's judges were tasked with implementing God's justice: *"It shall be life for life, eye for eye, tooth for tooth, hand for hand, foot for foot"* (Deuteronomy 19:21b). The result was that evil would be purged from Israel, and the people would fear God and live in peace.

Jesus mentioned this Old Testament law when He was teaching the Sermon on the Mount: Read His words in Matthew 5:38-39 and 43-46. How was Jesus' teaching even more radical than the Old Testament?

Following God and obeying His commandments brings the blessings of His peace and nearness. Even though we make mistakes, God, in His mercy, provides a place of refuge for us in Christ Jesus. By following Jesus, we can have abundant purpose and a life God will use for His glory.

Write out Philippians 3:13-14 in the space below, and meditate on these words of Paul that mirror God's compassion in Deuteronomy 19. Ask God to surround you with His compassion and guidance as you move forward in faith.

At times, we allow ourselves to believe we should be exempt from hardship and struggles because we are God's children. Studying the struggles and hardships of the children of Israel shows us we are not exempt, yet it also gives us courage in our journey.

God knew enemies would rise up against Israel. Although they would have to fight many battles, God promised to be with them and fight for them. We can take comfort that God is the same yesterday, today and forever, and He will be with us and fight for us against our enemies.

In Deuteronomy 20:1-4, why was Israel not to fear the coming battles against their enemies?

In verses 5-8, Moses lists some exemptions for men who would not be expected to go to battle for Israel. Fighting for Israel would take tremendous concentration, courage and skill.

Two types of warfare were outlined for Israel: one commanded by God (against the seven nations of Canaan [vv. 16-17]) and the other permitted by God (against those nations on the outer borders who might provoke or invade Israel [vv. 10-11]).

To all cities the Israelites would encounter on their outer borders, God commanded Israel to first

"offer terms of _____ *"* (Deuteronomy 20:10).

One of God's names is *Jehovah-Shalom*: "the Lord is peace." If the city accepted peace, all the residents would live as part of Israel, paying taxes and serving with Israel against future enemies. If not, they would be besieged. (v. 12)

These verses on warfare are difficult to explain in today's terms. In order to understand Deuteronomy 20, we must first place God where He belongs: on His throne as Creator and Sovereign over all. When His creation sins against Him, (Genesis 3) God's judgment follows because He cannot be in the presence of sin.

The Lord told Israel to completely destroy six nations. (Deuteronomy 20:16-18) Why?

God knew all the nations; He knew their hearts, and He knew their idolatrous practices. Because He loved Israel, He desired to protect them against cultures and ideas that would lead them away from Him. It was not because of Israel's own righteousness but because of the evil of these nations, and because of God's promise to Abraham, that the nations were destroyed. (Deuteronomy 9:5-6) Although all of these nations fell by Israel's swords, their destruction was accomplished by the divine hand of God.

Read verses 1 and 4 of Deuteronomy 20 again. What was the promise of God contained in these verses?

How do these verses give comfort and courage to you in the battles you are facing?

Map of the Nations of Canaan

THAT ISRAEL WAS TO DESTROY

Circle the areas of the map that represent the nations that Israel was to completely destroy according to Deuteronomy 20:17. How does this give you insight into the idolatry that engulfed Israel's new land?

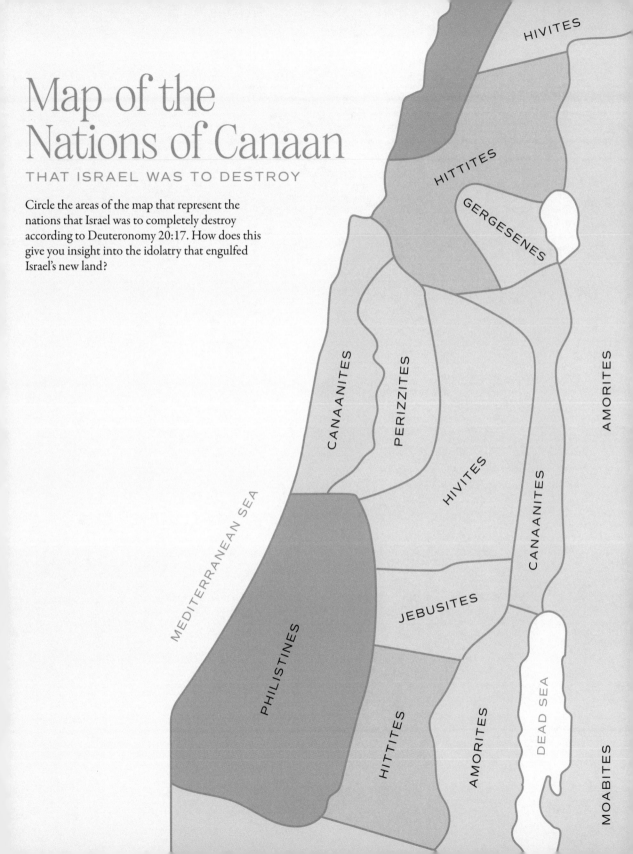

Feasts of God

	TIME OF YEAR	# OF DAYS	OFFERING
Passover and Unleavened Bread	Month of Abib: 14th day and following 7 days	7 days	Unblemished lamb; unleavened bread
Feast of Weeks (Pentecost)	Seven weeks after Passover and Feast of Unleavened Bread	7 days	New grain from the harvest and two loaves of bread (with leaven)
Feast of Booths (Feast of Tabernacles)	Immediately after the fall harvest	7 days	Food offering

PLACE	PURPOSE AND SIGNIFICANCE (OLD TESTAMENT)	PARALLEL SIGNIFICANCE IN THE NEW TESTAMENT
Jerusalem	A remembrance of the night the Lord "passed over" His people's homes, which were marked by lambs' blood, and delivered them out of bondage in Egypt to life and freedom as a new nation. The unleavened bread reminded them of the haste with which they left Egypt.	Passover was being celebrated in Jerusalem when Jesus, the Lamb of God, was crucified. His death and resurrection freed us from the bondage of sin to give us new and eternal life in Him. (1 Corinthians 5:7-8)
Jerusalem	Celebration of the spring grain harvest and remembrance of the giving of the Mosaic Covenant (Ten Commandments) on Mount Sinai. This was a feast of rejoicing for all the ways God had provided for His people. No one was to be excluded.	Fifty days after the resurrection of Christ, on Pentecost, God gave the Holy Spirit to those who believed. It was the new covenant of grace, which was poured out through His Spirit. (Acts 2: 1-4) This was a day of great rejoicing for all God had provided through Jesus Christ and the Holy Spirit.
Jerusalem	The people of Israel would construct "booths" for their families out of wood and straw to commemorate God's provision for them in the wilderness, where they lived in tents for 40 years before He brought them into the "land flowing with milk and honey." They also celebrated the fall harvest at this time, thanking God for His continued provision.	On the last day of this feast in Jerusalem, Jesus revealed Himself as the Messiah and offered the provision of living water through the indwelling presence of His Spirit to those who were His faithful followers. *"If anyone thirsts, let him come to me and drink. Whoever believes in me, as the Scripture has said, 'Out of his heart will flow rivers of living water.'"* (John 7:37-38)

Weekend *Reflection*

Looking back over Chapters 16-20 in Deuteronomy, we see God's heart for His people. We see His desire for them to remember where they had begun and who had led them. It was by God's mighty hand that:

- They were freed from the bondage of Egypt.
- For 40 years in a desert wasteland, their food, water and shelter were supernaturally provided.
- They were standing on the edge of the land God promised Abraham hundreds of years ago.

Everything good that had come to them was because of their God. They did nothing to earn or deserve His favor, yet He saved them. Why?

Because God desired a relationship with these people. God met all their physical needs — and gave them so much more. The Giver was actually the true Gift. The feasts He commanded were to remind them of the Giver.

Often we are tempted to be proud that God is a part of our story, but in reality, we are a part of His story. We did nothing to earn His favor or deserve His love. Only by His grace, He reached down to us, freed us from the bondage of sin and gave us new life through Christ. What a God! Obedience to His calling is the highest and best use of our lives, and as we obey we are blessed by the Giver, with the Gift — His presence.

PRAYER:

Dear Lord, we humble ourselves before You and thank You for drawing us into Your story. Thank you for the gift of salvation, the gift of knowing and serving You. We acknowledge You as the Giver. Help us to listen to Your voice, follow Your commands and love You with all of our hearts.

Lord, I pray Your words today from Deuteronomy 20:4:

"for the LORD your God is he who goes with you to fight for you against your enemies, to give you the victory."

In Jesus' name, amen.

Notes

Notes

Week
Five

Day 21

Moses addressed situations relating to several of the Ten Commandments.

It's amazing that the Lord provided guidance for all kinds of scenarios Israel might encounter as they entered the promised land. In this study we're not able to address every verse of Scripture in every chapter, but let's take a close look at two of the scenarios covered in Deuteronomy 21.

1. UNSOLVED MURDERS

In Deuteronomy 21:1-9, Moses addressed the sixth of the Ten Commandments: *"You shall not murder"* (Exodus 20:13). In Hebrew culture, murder was a crime punishable by death, and the sentence was always carried out swiftly to ensure the land was cleansed from the shedding of innocent blood.

> According to Deuteronomy 21, what was to be done if a person was found dead with no evidence of who commited the murder?

The slaying of the heifer (young female cow) was a request for atonement. By this act, all would understand the severity of the sin of murder.

> The death of the heifer would "_____ _____ _____ *of innocent blood*" (v. 9) before God.

2. A REBELLIOUS SON

The fifth of the Ten Commandments, *"Honor your father and your mother"* (Exodus 20:12), is also addressed here in Deuteronomy 21. God desired His people to raise up generations that would respect authority and know and follow Him.

> Flip back and read Deuteronomy 6:4-7. How were the children of Israel commanded to raise their children?

Parents who had done everything possible to bring a son to obedience were given instructions: If their son remained rebellious, he was brought before the rulers (elders) to decide his fate. If the rulers judged him to be a danger to the community, he was stoned to death. (Deuteronomy 21:18-21)

What was the reason for the severity of this punishment? (v. 21b)

Nine times in Deuteronomy, the phrase *"purge the evil"* is used. Each time, it refers to eliminating sin and unrepentance among God's people lest they follow the same path as the evildoer.[1]

Jesus told a parable about a rebellious son in Luke 15:11-31. What are the similarities and differences between the son in Deuteronomy 21 and the son in Luke 15?

According to Luke 15:21, what was the difference in the son's heart when he returned to his father?

How does the father's compassion in Luke 15:20-24 give you a better understanding of God as your Father?

Repentance not only brings reconciliation with God, but it also gives freedom to our souls. What the enemy seeks to destroy through sin in our lives, God seeks to repair and restore through repentance. Thank God today for His compassion, reconciliation and redemption.

Day 22

Details of various laws, including laws about sexual purity, were explained.

So many laws, so many details, so many specifics. Think of Moses having to write all these words for God's people. It may have been exhausting. But Moses knew these were not random laws given by an indifferent sovereign. ALL of the laws in Scripture are given by a loving God who desires peace and prosperity for His chosen people. Let's ask God to give us eyes to see His Word through the lens of His love and faithfulness toward Israel (and us) in these next chapters.

In verses 1-4 of Deuteronomy 22, Moses used the examples of wayward oxen and sheep to explain how Israelites were to love their brothers (fellow Israelites). Treating one another with respect, compassion and kindness would set apart God's people and allow them to be a light to other nations.

Read Deuteronomy 22:1-4. How might you translate this into everyday language? What is the main idea?

Read Mark 12:31 and compare Jesus' words with the laws above.

Next, the subject changes from neighborly relationships to intimate relationships. If we read Deuteronomy 22:13-30 through the lens of God's holiness and faithfulness, we are given insight into God's heart: Since marriage is a holy covenant, adultery is, in a way, analogous to idolatry and is forbidden by God. When God created man and woman, He designed them for sexual oneness only in sacred marriage. (Genesis 2:24) Knowing adultery would break apart the one-flesh relationship and cause tremendous emotional pain, God plainly commanded, *"You shall not commit adultery"* (Exodus 20:14). His laws reflected His desire that those of His people who were married would live in faithfulness (oneness) within marriage and faithfulness (oneness) with Him.

How have you seen the results of adultery breaking apart relationships and causing hurt in the lives of those you love?

Marriage is still a sacred covenant in the eyes of the Lord. According to Ephesians 5:31-32, what does marriage actually represent?

The mystery has been revealed: Every wedding ceremony is a picture of the Bridegroom being united with His Bride. Jesus is the Bridegroom, and the Church is His Bride. (Revelation 19:7) God's desire for marriage is that it would be an example to the watching world of His loving relationship to His people.

Though many people today agree adultery is wrong, God's laws on topics like sexual purity may sometimes seem outdated by our cultural norms. How can we contextualize the eternal principles of our God and focus our hearts to stand on His unchanging Word?

Day 23

Moses addressed laws regarding the assembly of the Lord, among other commands.

Focusing on "the letter of the law" often causes us to neglect the Giver of the law. While the specific laws and regulations concerning the assembly of the Lord can be confusing to us today, most Bible scholars agree the laws in Deuteronomy 23 were intended to discourage God's people from imitating the heathen nations surrounding them.[1] Their sacred gatherings before the Lord were to be free from moral, ceremonial and natural pollution.

Even though the cultural norms of 1300 B.C. were very different from our cultural norms today, God never changes. When we struggle to understand God's ways, we can choose to trust His heart. Let's look at three verses from this chapter that give insight into God's heart for His people's purity:

1.) Deuteronomy 23:5:

> "... THE LORD YOUR GOD TURNED THE _____
>
> INTO A _____ FOR YOU, BECAUSE THE
>
> LORD YOUR GOD _____ YOU."

The story of Balaam is found in Numbers 22-23. The wicked king of Moab ordered the false prophet Balaam to go and curse Israel so Moab could conquer them. On the way to Israel, God miraculously changed the message of Balaam from a curse to a blessing. (By the way, there is also a talking donkey in this story. It's worth the read!)

　　Why did God intervene on Israel's behalf?

2.) Deuteronomy 23:14:

> "BECAUSE THE LORD YOUR GOD WALKS _____ _____
>
> _____ OF YOUR CAMP, TO _____
>
> YOU AND TO GIVE UP YOUR ENEMIES BEFORE YOU,
>
> THEREFORE YOUR CAMP MUST BE HOLY ..."

Why would God desire holiness within the camp of His army?

3.) Deuteronomy 23:20:

> "... YOU MAY NOT CHARGE YOUR BROTHER INTEREST,
> THAT THE LORD YOUR GOD MAY _____ _____
> IN _____ THAT YOU UNDERTAKE IN THE LAND THAT
> YOU ARE ENTERING TO TAKE POSSESSION OF IT."

What is God's heart for His people according to this verse?

After thousands of years, God's heart for His people has not changed:

The Lord loves us. (1 John 4:16)
The Lord saves us so we may live for Him in holiness. (2 Corinthians 5:15)
The Lord desires to bless us. (Romans 8:28)

His laws are perfectly aligned with His loving plan to draw His people to Himself. As we trust His heart and obey His truths, our hearts are revived, and we are at peace.

Read Psalm 19:7, and write a brief prayer asking God to draw you closer to His heart.

Day 24

Laws were given to protect the poor and needy of Israel, and God told Israel to remember and destroy Amalek.

Compassion, mercy, justice: These are key attributes of the character of our God. Because of God's compassion for the needy and helpless of Israel, His people were to extend His compassion, mercy and justice to those in need.

In Deuteronomy 24, the Lord gave various laws to guarantee protection for those who might otherwise be neglected or exploited: for example, divorced women, poor borrowers, sojourners and servants. At all times Israelites were to be compassionate and merciful to the oppressed, remembering how Israel had felt when they were oppressed in Egypt. (Deuteronomy 24:17-18)

Moses reminded the people: *"you shall remember that you were a slave in Egypt and the LORD your God redeemed you from there"* (v. 18). Why would it be important for Israel to remember their slavery ... and their redemption?

How should remembering our bondage to sin — and our freedom in Christ — instill in us a sense of compassion toward those in need in our culture?

Read Matthew 25:34-40. How were Jesus' words about those in need similar to the words spoken by Moses to the children of Israel?

make it count

Deuteronomy 24:19-21 mentions three groups of people whom Israelites were to remember when they harvested grain, olives and grapes. What were the three classes of people, and how was Israel to provide for them?

Ask the Lord to help you identify someone in your community who is in need and how you can help them. Write their name(s) here:

Deuteronomy 25 also addressed laws for handling disputes between individuals in Israel. In every situation addressed, Moses spoke wisdom for life from the One who created life.

Finally, in verse 17 God commanded Israel,

"REMEMBER WHAT _____ DID TO YOU ON

THE WAY AS YOU CAME OUT OF EGYPT..."

Read the story of the Amalekites in Exodus 17:8-14. How do verses 17-18 of Deuteronomy 25 give greater insight into Amalek's wickedness?

Bible scholar Charles Spurgeon has made a correlation between Amalek and sin. Sin, like Amalek, is a powerful enemy; it attacks us at the most vulnerable point and is set on destroying God's people.[1]

How are Paul's words in Romans 6:11, regarding our sin, similar to God's words about Amalek in Deuteronomy 25:19?

Day 25

Moses commanded Israel to give their best to the Lord and obey Him with all their hearts and souls.

The phrase *"the LORD your God"* is used five times in the first four verses of Deuteronomy 26. Why was this important for Israel to remember? Through this phrase, Moses emphasized that YAHWEH (the I AM of Exodus 3:14) was THEIR God. They were about to experience the fulfillment of all God's promises, and their God would continue to provide.

All Israelites were commanded to bring offerings of their first fruits (the best of their crops) to the altar of God as a tithe from His provision, reciting the story of Israel before the priest to remind them of their humble beginnings as slaves in Egypt.

Read Deuteronomy 26:5-10 and list God's provisions for His people.

According to verses 10-11, what was to be the attitude of the people's hearts as they came before the Lord their God?

Why is it important for you, too, to *"rejoice in all the good that the LORD your God has given to you"* (v. 11)?

Part of the tithe brought to the temple would be used to feed those serving as priests (Aaron's descendants in the tribe of Levi) and the needy — including orphans, widows and sojourners.

How do our tithes and offerings work in similar ways today?

In verse 16, Moses encouraged his people not just to obey these statutes outwardly but also to be *"careful to do them with <u>all your heart</u> and with <u>all your soul</u>."*

Compare Deuteronomy 26:16 with John 14:15 and Matthew 22:37. What words and thoughts of Moses and Jesus are similar?

Why is God concerned about obedience that emanates from our hearts?

The depth of God's love for His people was revealed through Moses' words about Israel as *"a people for his treasured possession"* (Deuteronomy 26:18).

Read Deuteronomy 26:18-19, and compare it with the Apostle Paul's words in Titus 2:14, describing why Jesus gave Himself for us:

"TO _____ US FROM ALL LAWLESSNESS

AND TO _____ FOR HIMSELF A

_____ FOR HIS OWN _____ WHO

ARE ZEALOUS FOR GOOD WORKS."

To think we are God's own treasured possession is unfathomable. Read back through the verses mentioned in this lesson, asking God to speak His words of life, love and redemption to your heart.

Weekend *Reflection*

In His wisdom, God gave His people an instruction manual for how to live. Often we think of the Ten Commandments as God's official instructions for life, and they are that; however, God also elaborated on these 10 laws to address specific situations, and the book of Deuteronomy answers many how-to-implement questions for God's laws.

God had a purpose and design in creation. When we seek to understand the words of Deuteronomy through the eyes of our divine Creator, the words are not demands made by an impersonal sovereign, but instead they are life-giving instructions to benefit us, His creation.

In the pages of Deuteronomy, we uncover the heart of God: His heart of love, compassion and relationship. God wanted His people's hearts to mirror His heart. Moses told the people to keep God's laws *"with all your heart and with all your soul"* (Deuteronomy 26:16).

Obedience to God in ancient Israel meant His presence, peace and prosperity. God still desires obedience from the hearts of His people today, not to fulfill the law but to express gratitude that Jesus has fulfilled it. The abundance of life comes from surrendering to the One who is the Giver of abundant life. In Him we find our joy; in Him we find our peace, and it is in surrender to Him that we find freedom to live with purpose.

PRAYER:

Dear Lord, I surrender to You and to Your way for my life. I want to live with purpose, knowing You have made me for a purpose. Give me the courage and strength to obey You with everything that is in me. Let me recognize and fight against my tendency to rebel and go my own way. Guide my every step with Your grace. Let my life be a light to others that they may see Your love, kindness, goodness and mercy through me.

Lord, I pray Your words today from Deuteronomy 26:16:

"This day the LORD your God commands you to do these statutes and rules. You shall therefore be careful to do them with all your heart and with all your soul."

In Jesus' name, amen.

Notes

Notes

Week
Six

Day 26

DEUTERONOMY 27

Moses commanded Israel to remember God, and the covenant curses were revealed.

Over and over in the book of Deuteronomy, Moses encouraged the people to remember and obey God's commands. In Deuteronomy 27:1-5, Moses told them that once they entered the promised land, they were to write the law on plastered stones, set the stones on Mount Ebal, erect an altar there, offer sacrifices and rejoice before the Lord. All these actions would help Israel remember and obey God's commands.

Verses 9-10 are key to understanding this chapter:

> "... THIS DAY YOU HAVE BECOME THE PEOPLE OF THE LORD YOUR GOD. YOU SHALL THEREFORE _____ _____ _____ OF THE LORD YOUR GOD, _____ HIS COMMANDMENTS AND HIS STATUTES, WHICH I COMMAND YOU TODAY."

This is the language of covenant between God (the Sovereign) and His people (the subjects of His Kingdom). As chosen and delivered by the eternal God, Israel was to be faithful to Him, their Sovereign, just as He had been faithful to them.

This covenant was similar to ancient Near Eastern treaties in which the actions to be performed — and avoided — were listed. (Remember how we learned about Near East Suzerain Treaty Patterns on page 11?) Also, blessings for conformity and curses for nonconformity would be detailed in these documents.[1] In Deuteronomy 27:15-26, Moses listed the behavior that would bring God's curses upon His people.

Compare verses 15-26 with the Ten Commandments. (Exodus 20:3-17)

Today, God does not ask us to write His words on stones, but we still need to remember and be faithful to His commands. Read Psalm 119:11. Where should God's words be kept?

For believers, God has removed our hearts of stone, giving us hearts of flesh, (Ezekiel 36:26) and has written His law on our hearts. (Jeremiah 31:33) What is one step you can take to apply these verses in your life today?

Note that most of the curses in Deuteronomy 27 related to sins committed in secret. God wanted Israel to know His watchful eye sees even those things that are hidden from man.

But curses of God are not discussed much in Christian circles today ... because of Jesus. Jesus absorbed the curse of God for the sins of the world as He suffered and died on Calvary's cross. *"Christ redeemed us from the curse of the law by becoming a curse for us ..."* (Galatians 3:13) The debt we owed for our sins was paid, the wrath of God satisfied, the curse removed and righteousness freely bestowed. Praise God — through faith, we have been freed from the curse of sin!

Write out 1 Peter 2:24 in the space below, and offer a prayer of thanksgiving to God for all Jesus did for you on the cross.

Day 27

DEUTERONOMY 28:1-14
Moses explained the covenant blessings for obedience.

The children of Israel must have been delighted with Moses' words of blessings: God was promising to protect, provide and give them every form of prosperity. They only needed to live in obedience to His commands. It sounded so simple.

How does Deuteronomy 28:2 speak of the abundance God desired to lavish on His children?

Read Deuteronomy 28:3-14 and the blessings Israel would receive if they obeyed God's commands. Which blessings stand out the most to you?

In Deuteronomy 28:12b, notice the words *"and you shall lend to many nations."* God's blessing on Israel would not only be for them but also for <u>other nations</u> to be blessed through Israel.

How was God using Israel to fulfill His oath to Abraham? (See Genesis 26:4.)

According to Deuteronomy 28:13-14, what were two requirements necessary for Israel to receive all the blessings promised by God?

Why would anyone **not** want to follow this amazing God, this God who is in control of both nature and nations, this God who desires to shower His people with abundance and blessings?

But even while these material blessings mentioned in Deuteronomy 28 are good, and all good things come from God, Jesus shows us obedience to Him may also be costly. (Luke 9:23) As we identify ourselves with Jesus and follow after Him, we release ourselves from the mentality of expecting God's blessings to come wrapped in the trappings of this world.

Use the following verses to explain a few of the intangible blessings of God:

1 PETER 1:3-4

ROMANS 8:11

EPHESIANS 1:3

As we come to know God, love Him and serve Him, we find we want to know Him, love Him and serve Him more and more ... and the cycle of obedience and blessing takes root in the life of a believer. As He fills our lives, we are able to fill the lives of others: The blessed become the blessing.

How can you be a blessing to someone today?

Day 28

DEUTERONOMY 28:15-68
More covenant curses for disobedience were given.

The inevitable result of forsaking the one true God, turning to the gods of Canaan, would be disastrous for Israel. Breaking covenant with God would result in the removal of God's protection and favor, and forfeiture of all God's promised abundance spoken of in the preceding verses.

Compare Deuteronomy 28:1 and verse 15. What is the key difference between these verses?

In verse 20, Moses interjected a phrase from the Lord as to why the people would suffer the curses:

"... ON ACCOUNT OF THE _____ ____

_____ _____ , BECAUSE YOU HAVE

_____ ME."

God promised He would never turn away from Israel, unless they turned away from Him.
Read verses 21-27 and list some of the ways God would judge a disobedient Israel.

Note that the list of curses was comprehensive: famine, diseases, pestilence, loss of prosperity and loss of the land — the good land God provided.

Verses 29 and 31 end with the same ominous phrase:

"THERE SHALL BE ____ _____ TO _____ _____."

Idols made of metal, wood and stone had no power, and if Israel trusted in those idols, the presence and power of the living God would no longer be available to save them.

In verses 45 and 47, Moses gave two scenarios that would cause Israel to experience the curses of God:

DEUTERONOMY 28:45 —

DEUTERONOMY 28:47 —

Sin always has consequences. How are the consequences of our sin, according to Romans 6:23, similar to the consequences of Israel's sin? (Note that "death" means both bodily mortality and *spiritual separation from God.*)

We have all sinned and fallen short of His perfection. (Romans 3:23) But God, in His grace, sent Jesus to take our sin and our punishment on the cross so we could experience God's blessing of abundant life forever.

Still, today human nature has not changed. Although we should desire to obey God and walk with Him, the shiny objects of the world are so tempting.

Is there any area of your life in which you have forsaken God and need His forgiveness? Talk to God about it. *"Draw near to God, and he will draw near to you."* (James 4:8)

Day 29

God renewed His covenant just before Israel entered the promised land.

God desired to restore His relationship with humanity, which had been broken in the garden of Eden. The covenant that God established at Mount Sinai in Exodus was part of the beginning of God drawing His people back into relationship, and the covenant at Moab was a renewal of the Sinai covenant.

Only two people in the congregation who had witnessed God's covenant at Mount Sinai — Caleb and Joshua (Numbers 14:30) — were still alive when Israel stood ready to cross the Jordan River on the plains of Moab in Deuteronomy 29. Because of God's great love and faithfulness to His people, He desired for everyone to hear His heart once more before they entered the promised land. Notice Moses gathered ALL of Israel together. (Deuteronomy 29:2)

First, Moses recounted the signs and wonders God had performed during their journey in the wilderness. The Israelites were there only by the power, provision and grace of God.

Read Deuteronomy 29:2-8. List some provisions of God's grace in these verses.

Besides the people of Israel, who was included in God's covenant? (See verses 11 and 15.)

How would you have felt if you belonged to one of the groups mentioned above?

The language of this covenant is the language of love and relationship. Israel's rebellion in the wilderness could have been the end of their nation; however, God loved them and forgave them. Leaving behind their past, the Israelites were looking forward to God's blessings in their future home. And to keep God's covenant, Israel owed Him their faithfulness and obedience.

Read Deuteronomy 29:29. Why had God chosen to reveal His words to Israel?

The covenants at Mount Sinai and Moab were a foreshadowing of a future covenant — the covenant that would be ushered in by the obedience of Jesus. His *"obedien[ce] to the point of death, even death on a cross"* (Philippians 2:8) on our behalf allows us to be righteous before God. (Philippians 3:9)

Compare the *prophecy* of the new covenant in Jeremiah 31:31-33 with the *fulfillment* of the new covenant through Jesus in Luke 22:20 and Colossians 1:19-20.

According to Deuteronomy 29, verses 18, 25 and 26, what actions would break God's covenant and bring about God's wrath?

Jesus never turned away from any of God's commands. Yet who turned away from Him on the cross? (Matthew 27:46) Why?

Fire, cloud and miraculous deeds were God's messengers of revelation to the Israelites; however, the most incredible miracle and messenger of God is Jesus Christ. God became like us so that we can be like Him: *"in Christ God was reconciling the world to himself"* (2 Corinthians 5:19).

How and when did God reach you and bring you to Himself?

Day 30

DEUTERONOMY 30

Moses prophesied Israel's rebellion and repentance and God's restoration.

Remarkably, despite all of the warnings of the consequences listed in the previous chapter, Moses prophesied Israel would still in fact break the covenant! (Deuteronomy 30:1)

Israel's pursuit of other gods would bring the curses for disobedience, and they would be exiled to other nations; however, because of His great love, God would draw Israel to repentance and restore them to their land.

Read Deuteronomy 30, verses 10, 16 and 20. What similar words/phrases were used by Moses to remind Israel of their responsibility to God's covenant?

Read 2 Chronicles 7:14. How does this verse give you a better understanding of God's compassion for His wayward people?

The command to obey God was not complicated; it was clear and simple. Love and obedience would lead to life and prosperity while self-will and disobedience would lead to adversity and death. And yet ...

Moses spoke of a time in Israel's future when:

"THE LORD YOUR GOD WILL CIRCUMCISE YOUR

_____ AND THE _____ OF YOUR

OFFSPRING, SO THAT YOU WILL LOVE THE LORD

YOUR GOD WITH ALL YOUR _____ AND WITH

ALL YOUR _____, THAT YOU MAY LIVE."

DEUTERONOMY 30:6

"Circumcision of the heart" meant someday the sin nature (of Adam) would be cut away so the hearts of God's people would be free to love God fully. That could never be possible without Jesus. Jesus lived a perfect life and, as the spotless Lamb of God, offered up His life as a sacrifice for our sins. (John 1:29) As we put our faith in Him, the "flesh" of our hearts is circumcised (cut away) so we may live by faith. (Colossians 2:11) He releases us from the power of sin, and His resurrection gives us life abundantly on this earth (John 10:10) and eternally with Him. (1 John 2:25)

Obedience to the law is necessary, yet it is impossible for us to obey perfectly. God's law was given to point us to our sin. It also points us to our need for a Savior: the One whom God would send to rescue all people from the curse of sin.

Read Galatians 3:21. What does this verse tell us about righteousness under the law versus righteousness by faith?

In Deuteronomy 30:19, Moses set before Israel a choice between life and death, the blessing and the curse. Then he told them to *choose life!*

There was no mystery in how this was to be accomplished, as Moses made it perfectly clear in verse 20. How would Israel choose life?

Like Israel, we have a choice each day: Will we love God with all our hearts and hold fast to Him? Or will we choose our own path and turn away from Him? In Romans 7, Paul described the tension, which exists in every believer, between our sinful flesh and our desire to serve the Lord. One day, we will be freed from the presence and the power of sin, but until that day, we rely on Jesus — one day at a time. He is the One who is able to give us all we need to live for Him.

Write out 2 Peter 1:3. How do these words give you hope?

Weekend *Reflection*

Israel's choice was simple: Choose LIFE. The way was simple: Obey God's commands with all their hearts and all their souls. That phrase *"with all your heart and all your soul"* is found again and again in Deuteronomy. It was so simple ... but it wasn't easy.

It wasn't easy for Israel, and it's not easy for us — in fact, it's impossible to obey God perfectly. Our sinful nature, inherited through Adam, is within all of us and is stubborn and wicked, desiring to exalt self rather than God. This is why we needed Jesus, our sinless Savior, to live, die and rise again in perfect obedience *for us.*

When reading Deuteronomy 27-30, we see God's heart for frail humans. God's heart is revealed through His covenant: He would be Israel's God, and they would be *"a people for His treasured possession"* (Deuteronomy 26:18). We see His great love for them, His desire to bless them and give them good things, to protect them and prosper them. And yet God knew the stubbornness of their hearts and their tendency to be lured into the idolatry of nations around them.

God's compassion, mercy and grace were always there for Israel, and He is always there for us. Coming to God is simple: *"Believe in the LORD Jesus, and you will be saved ..."* (Acts 16:31). Following God and serving Him is simple; but it is not easy. Loving God with all our hearts and all our souls involves surrender of our wills to the Creator. Those who choose to live in obedience to the Lord choose LIFE. And that LIFE in Christ is better than any life we could ever imagine without Him.

PRAYER:

Dear Lord, I want to love You with all my heart and all my soul. I want to serve You and follow You. Forgive me for allowing my eyes and my heart to be drawn to the "other gods" of this world. I desire the blessing of Your presence in my life. The "blessings" of this world are so temporary compared to the eternal blessings You offer. Help me to choose life — the abundant life You offer through Jesus — one day at a time.

Lord, I pray Your words today from Deuteronomy 30:19:

"I call heaven and earth to witness against you today, that I have set before you life and death, blessing and curse. Therefore choose life, that you and your offspring may live..."

In Jesus' name, amen.

Notes

Notes

Week
Seven

Day 31

DEUTERONOMY 31:1-13

Moses encouraged Israel and Joshua.

The people of Israel must have been shocked and fearful as Moses explained they would enter the promised land without him. Moses had been their faithful leader for 40 years — from slavery in Egypt to the edge of their new home. Knowing the people needed encouragement, he pointed to God's past faithfulness and also to His future plans to bless them.

Besides Joshua, who did Moses say would go before them — and with them — as they entered the land? (See verses 3 and 6.)

Read Deuteronomy 31:6-8. List the four phrases that appear in both Moses' charge to the people (v. 6) AND Moses' charge to Joshua. (vv. 7-8)

Meditate on these words for a few minutes and recite them over your heart today.

After speaking to the people, Moses finished writing the record of God's law. His assignment was done; every word commanded by God was written on the scroll of Israel. Can you imagine the responsibility of writing all of God's words — for 40 years? This manuscript would be kept by the priests of Israel in the most sacred place, next to the Ark of the Covenant. (v. 9)

The written words of God were to be the absolute standard of reference in all matters of life, conduct and justice for the nation of Israel for generations to come. At the end of every seven years, during the Feast of Booths (which we learned about on Day 16 of this study), all the tribes of Israel from the various lands God had given them would come together at the tabernacle in Jerusalem. They would all listen as the entire law was read. (v. 11)

What was the reading of the law designed to accomplish? (v. 12)

According to verse 13, why was God concerned about the generations to come in Israel?

How does reading and memorizing Scripture with the children in your family or church encourage them (and you) to love God and serve Him faithfully?

Day 32

DEUTERONOMY 31:14-29
Joshua was commissioned, and Israel's future was prophesied.

It was imperative for the children of Israel to know that just as Moses had been appointed by God to lead His people out of Egypt, Joshua had been appointed by God to lead them into Canaan. God thereby summoned Moses and Joshua to appear before Him at the tabernacle. The pillar of cloud was God's sign to His people that God Himself was the One commissioning Joshua as His chosen leader of Israel.

Read Deuteronomy 31:16 and verse 20. What were Moses and Joshua told regarding Israel's future?

How could a people who had been promised the blessings of life and prosperity turn away from the very Giver of life and prosperity? The answer is found in one word: SIN.

Their fallen, sinful nature twisted their thoughts and turned their focus from God onto themselves. This would be the downfall of Israel.

Once again, Moses used the language of adultery to describe the idolatry Israel would pursue. Their actions would not only break God's covenant, but they would also break His heart.

Why do you think idolatry is such a serious offense against God? (If you need some help, you can flip back to Exodus 20:2-5.)

Deuteronomy 31:20 encapsulates God's prophecy of the progression of Israel's future. In this one verse, we see the faithfulness of God to His promises and His covenant, as well as Israel's selfishness and unfaithfulness to the God who had given them everything.

God said:

"FOR _____ __ _____ _____ THEM INTO THE

LAND FLOWING WITH MILK AND HONEY, WHICH ____

_____ __ _____ TO THEIR FATHERS, AND THEY

HAVE EATEN AND ARE FULL AND GROWN FAT, THEY

WILL TURN TO OTHER GODS AND SERVE THEM, AND

DESPISE ME AND BREAK MY COVENANT" (V. 20).

How do God's words from the above text reveal His heart?

Read Deuteronomy 31:27-29. What do you think was going through Moses' mind as he handed the baton of leadership to Joshua?

Sin is subtle, and we must be alert, aware and equipped with the Word of God to stand firm against the temptation to wander from the Lord or pursue the things of the world.

Read 1 John 2:15-17. How are these verses similar to the story of the Israelites?

When we focus our attention on God, how does it change our perspective on sin?

Do you think it was discouraging for Israel to be told, without a doubt, they would stumble in their sin? How do you fight any discouragement knowing you, too, will sin? (Hint: See 1 John 1:6-9.)

Day 33

God gave Moses a song of remembrance for Israel.

The Song of Moses in Deuteronomy 32 is actually a song composed by God. In Deuteronomy 31:19, the Lord told Moses to write this song and teach it to all of Israel. Aware of the people's tendency toward rebellion, God knew this song would be a reminder, for generations to come, that keeping His law would bring prosperity and blessings, but unfaithfulness would bring adversity.

To give you an idea of the significance of this song, there are 20 different psalms that quote words from the Song of Moses, and it is referenced over 28 times in the books of the Prophets in Scripture. There are also at least six references to it in the New Testament, in Philippians (2:15), Romans (10:19; 12:19; 15:10) and Hebrews (1:6; 10:30).

Read Deuteronomy 32:3-18 and compare God's character and His ways with Israel's ways.

GOD'S WAYS	ISRAEL'S WAYS
1.	1.
2.	2.
3.	3.
4.	4.
5.	5.

With which of Israel's sins can you most identify?

Despite your sin, how have you experienced God's compassion, provision and protection in the past?

Time after time, Israel's stubbornness and selfishness led to rebellion. Prosperity led them to forget their God and worship *"new gods"* (v. 17); therefore, in His righteous anger, God punished them. (vv. 19-25) In His perfect sovereignty, God would have compassion on them and draw them back to Himself. (v. 36) Each time Israel strayed, they would eventually repent and return to Yahweh, and He would heal them. (v. 43)

Moses summarized the law of God by saying:

"FOR IT IS NO _____ WORD FOR YOU,

BUT YOUR _____ _____ ..."

DEUTERONOMY 32:47

God's law was the standard for their lives, but no one would ever be able to keep all the laws perfectly — until Jesus came. In Galatians 3:10-12, the Apostle Paul encouraged his fellow believers to remember it is not our works (attempts to follow the law) but our faith in Christ that gives us right standing before God. Because Jesus kept the law for us, He is able to give us His eternal life.

Whether in ancient Israel or today, God's words are life because they point us to faith in the promised seed of Abraham, to Christ and His righteousness!

Read Hebrews 4:12 and explain how the Word of God works in our lives today just as it did in Israel thousands of years ago.

As you consider the Song of Moses, ask the Lord to give you eyes to see His greatness and glory ... and to understand His heart for His people through these verses.

Day 34

Moses called the tribes of Israel together to bless them.

In ancient times, it was customary for a father to gather his sons and bless each one before the father died. Knowing he had only a few days left on earth, Moses gathered the sons (tribes) of Israel together and spoke a blessing over each one. Notice that every time Moses spoke to the people in these last few chapters of Deuteronomy, he began by reminding them of God's faithfulness.

In verse 4, the law given at Mount Sinai is referred to as *"a possession for the assembly of Jacob."* It was imperative for Israel to understand that God's law was an inheritance given to Israel because of His love. In verse 5, Moses refers to the Lord as *"king in Jeshurun."* As we mentioned on Day 33, the name "Jeshurun" means *upright one* or *beloved one* and was a term of affection for Israel.[1]

What does it tell you about God that He called Israel (Jeshurun) "upright" and "beloved" even though the people had sinned against Him?

According to 2 Corinthians 5:21, how does God consider us upright or righteous today, even though we, like Israel, have been sinful?

Moses spoke prophetic blessings individually over each of the tribes of Israel. Let's look at two of the blessings.

Read Moses' blessing of Judah in Deuteronomy 33:7. Moses beseeched God to

" _____, O LORD, THE VOICE OF JUDAH" AND

"BE A _____ AGAINST HIS ADVERSARIES."

Judah would be the center of Israel's leadership. Israel's kings would descend from this tribe and reign from Jerusalem. Judah would lead Israel to battle against its enemies. And Jesus Christ's lineage would come through the tribe of Judah; thus He is referred to in Revelation 5:5 as the *"Lion of the tribe of Judah."*

Deuteronomy 33:12 is Moses' blessing on the tribe of Benjamin:

"THE _____ ____ ____ _____

DWELLS IN SAFETY. THE HIGH GOD

_____ _____ ALL DAY LONG ..."

These phrases had significance because the tabernacle of God would be located in the land of Benjamin; therefore, a unique manifestation of the Lord's presence and protection would be with Benjamin's tribe. The next phrase, *"and dwells between his shoulders,"* speaks to the tenderness of the Lord carrying Benjamin as a shepherd would carry a lamb (v. 12).

Lastly, Moses blessed all of Israel with powerful imagery of the God he knew so well. Read Deuteronomy 33:26-29 and list some of the images of God.

Have you ever pictured God *"rid[ing] through the heavens to your help"* (v. 26)? What do you need God to help you with today, and how does this image strengthen you to live with purpose as you await His help?

Write a prayer of gratitude to God using one of the images of God in verses 26-29, thanking Him for who He is.

Day 35

DEUTERONOMY 34

After meeting God at the top of Mount Nebo, Moses died.

On this final day of our study, we see Moses died just as he lived — in obedience and faith. Though his obedience was imperfect and sometimes doubt-filled, (Exodus 3:11; Exodus 5:22-23) after 40 years of walking through the desert with God and the people of Israel, his mission was complete.

Why did Moses go to Mount Nebo? (See Deuteronomy 32:48-50.)

Mount Nebo is over 2,600 feet above sea level.[1] Why do you think God took him to the top of this mountain in particular? (See Deuteronomy 34:1-4.)

Put your feet in the dirt of this story, and visualize the tour God gave Moses of the promised land. Scholars suggest Moses was fully capable of seeing all the glory of the amazing land God had promised. One commentator writes, "This view Moses had of the good land a little before his death may be an emblem of that sight believers have, by faith, of the heavenly glory, and which sometimes is the clearest when near to death."[2]

Although it had been over 450 years since the Lord had first promised Abraham this land for his offspring, God had not forgotten His promise.

Read Numbers 20:7-12. Why was Moses not allowed to enter the promised land?

Willful disobedience to God has consequences, and Moses accepted the consequences of his disobedience. But embedded in the verses of this chapter, we find a sweetness about Moses' death: He was in the presence of the Lord when he died, and the Lord Himself buried him! (Deuteronomy 34:5-6)

Use the following verses to describe the relationship between God and Moses.

DEUTERONOMY 34:10-11 —

EXODUS 33:7-11 —

All of Israel mourned for Moses. According to verses 11-12, they remembered all the *"signs and the wonders"* the Lord performed through Moses in Egypt and his *"mighty power and all the great deeds."* Moses was a man who knew God and trusted Him by faith. (See "The Miracles God Sent Moses To Do" on page 131)

Read the description of Moses' faith in Hebrews 11:24-27, and compare it to Paul's words about his faith in Philippians 3:7-9.

How would you describe your own faith in Jesus?

Friend, I pray your faith has grown stronger and deeper through our study of Deuteronomy.

We've learned so much about how ...

God desires to bless His people.

God desires that His people be faithful and obedient to His laws, which are given to protect and benefit them.

God fulfilled His promises in bringing His people to the edge of the promised land despite their rebellious past.

Israel, like us, continued to be stubborn and rebellious.

The final fulfillment of God's law is Jesus Christ: Through faith in Him, we are no longer bound by the power of sin or the letter of the law.

Deuteronomy reminds us that wherever we are in life, wherever we are in our walk of faith, we do not have to let our past define us. God has created us for a purpose, and we can move forward in faith.

What is one step you can take to move forward in faith today?

The Miracles God Sent Moses To Do

Weekend *Reflection*

As a parent, I want to shield my children and grandchildren from the difficult places in life. Because I love them and they are my people, I want them to make good choices, follow the Lord and serve Him faithfully. This was Moses' heart for his people. He loved them and wanted them to prosper in the beautiful land God had so graciously provided. But Moses also knew the stubborn, selfish, rebellious nature in their hearts. If we are honest with ourselves, we know those same tendencies dwell in our hearts.

What foolish creatures we are when we decide we know what is best for our lives rather than yielding to the almighty God who created us. We cannot live faithfully without living intentionally ... with our eyes set on Jesus. The Lord's desire is that we would experience the same face-to-face friendship with Him that Moses experienced. (Numbers 12:8) Moses knew his God, and Moses finished faithfully. I want that for my life — to know my God and finish faithfully.

Placing our faith in the Lord gives us courage to face the future because our life in Christ is secured by the cross. We could ask for no better security.

PRAYER:

Dear Lord, thank You for the example of Moses' life. Give us hearts that desire to be obedient to Your call, souls that long to love You, and minds that seek to know You. We confess our past sins and poor choices, and today, by the power of Your Holy Spirit, we choose to follow You faithfully. We want to live and die in obedience, just as Moses did. We want to be an example to the watching world that You are real, You are powerful and we can know You!

Lord, I pray Your words today from Deuteronomy 33:26-27a:

"There is none like God, O Jeshurun,
who rides through the heavens to your help,
through the skies in his majesty.
The eternal God is your dwelling place,
and underneath are the everlasting arms."

In Jesus' name, amen.

You Were Wondering:

01.

SHARON
BOLLINGER

"You shall not be partial in judgment. You shall hear the small and the great alike. You shall not be intimidated by anyone, for the judgment is God's. And the case that is too hard for you, you shall bring to me, and I will hear it." (Deuteronomy 1:17)

Deuteronomy, the second giving of the law — a kind of "masterclass" in Godly Leadership 101 — recalls the Lord's making of new leaders in Israel and a new generation proverbially attending the Wilderness School of God. The syllabus' opening point: Leaders are called to invest in new leaders.

Jethro, Moses' father-in-law, had offered Moses wise instruction about *"look[ing] for able men from all the people, men who fear God, who are trustworthy and hate a bribe, and plac[ing] such men over the people"* (Exodus 18:21). We see how this lesson was implemented in Deuteronomy 1. Moses trained up judges and leaders, trusted them and delegated responsibilities; he led by example in appointing tribal judges.

Justice is an attribute of God we are all called to model, and as such the judges Moses appointed were called to be righteous and not partial. Listening was essential. They were to exude no prejudice and deem every matter, *"the small and the great,"* important — all with God's Word as the foundational bedrock, appropriately fearing His righteous judgment. Their example of leadership teaches us to know our limits, slay pride, and seek spiritual counsel for wisdom, truth and discernment when *"the case... is too hard"* (v. 17).

02.

SANDY JOHNSON

"Only take care, and keep your soul diligently, lest you forget the things that your eyes have seen, and lest they depart from your heart all the days of your life. Make them known to your children and your children's children ..." (Deuteronomy 4:9)

Be careful! Watch out! Pay attention! Don't forget! These solemn warnings can be found throughout the book of Deuteronomy as Moses encouraged the Israelites to remember God's law. Here in verse 9, Moses pleaded with the people not to forget all God had done for them — *"the things that your eyes have seen."* Here are just a few of the miracles the Israelites would have witnessed: the 10 plagues in Egypt, (Exodus 7:20-12:30) the pillar of cloud and fire, (Exodus 13:21) the parting of the Red Sea, (Exodus 14) the provision of daily manna for food, (Exodus 16:14-35) and water from rocks. (Exodus 17:5-7; Numbers 20:7-11)

It seems like all those things would be easy to remember, right? But Moses knew how easily the people were prone to forgetting God and turning to idolatry, so he charged the Israelites not only to remember all God had done but also to teach their children and grandchildren. By passing along their history, future generations would learn about God's faithfulness and follow His commandments as well.

03.

VERA CHRISTIAN

"Know therefore today, and lay it to your heart, that the LORD is God in heaven above and on the earth beneath; there is no other." (Deuteronomy 4:39)

As this new generation of Israel reviewed their history and before they committed themselves anew to God's covenant for their generation, Moses wanted them to remember one irrefutable truth: The Lord, Yahweh, is the only God in heaven and on earth. Unlike all false gods, He is both transcendent and immanent, ruling sovereignly from heaven and yet present on earth, near in the midst of trouble. No other nation had a God like Israel's.

This is the same God we worship today. As we anticipate the promised land before us, we are tempted to pursue idols: success, health, reputation, comfort. Or perhaps what God asks us to do seems impossible and the enemies fierce. But the same God of Israel is our God. He is transcendent in heaven and immanent on earth. We can recommit afresh to trust Him in obedience, trusting He will fulfill His purposes as He fights alongside us.

04.

JEN ALLEE

"Oh that they had such a heart as this always, to fear me and to keep all my commandments, that it might go well with them and with their descendants forever!" (Deuteronomy 5:29)

The delivery of the Ten Commandments on Mount Sinai was for the benefit of the Israelites, and this heartfelt declaration from God explains why. Before Moses ascended the mountain, the people gathered near, per God's instructions, to witness His presence. Trumpets blared through thunder, lightning and a mysterious smoke-filled cloud, causing the Israelites to stand smartly at attention. Once the commands had been declared, the people quickly pleaded with Moses to remove them from God's presence, lest they be killed. (Deuteronomy 5:25-26) They pledged allegiance to God but begged for Moses to be their sole communicator. Yet God's presence, which inspired fearful awe in the people, was crucial to their obedience. Without a reverent fear of Him, the Israelites would easily put other gods before Him. They needed the holiness of God to motivate them to choose the path that was ultimately in their favor. Therefore, God tenderly urged them to keep this holy moment close to their hearts, knowing it was key to their success.

05.

SHARON BOLLINGER

"The LORD your God will raise up for you a prophet like me from among you, from your brothers—it is to him you shall listen ... I will raise up for them a prophet like you from among their brothers. And I will put my words in his mouth, and he shall speak to them all that I command him." (Deuteronomy 18:15, 18)

In Hebrew, *nabi* means "spokesman/speaker" and comes from *naba*, meaning "prophesy" or "to pour forth words abundantly." God's messenger and declarer of His will would speak words divinely received. Moses was such a messenger, a faithful servant and prophet, who gave Israel a glimpse of the coming Christ, testifying to the things that were to be spoken later. (Hebrews 3:5)

Moses' proclamations, and those of his prophetic successors, starting with Joshua, had greater implications than Israel could have comprehended in this threshold moment between the wilderness and Canaan. The promise of a greater Prophet was ultimately fulfilled by Jesus Christ, God's Word, (John 1:1) who was faithful to the Father who appointed Him to be poured out abundantly for all mankind. Moses' prophecy still resounds, as John 1:45 says, *"We have found him of whom Moses in the Law and also the prophets wrote, Jesus of Nazareth, the son of Joseph."* John 6:14 echoes, *"This is indeed the Prophet who is to come into the world!"*

06.
JILL BOYD

"Hear, O Israel: The LORD our God, the LORD is one. You shall love the LORD your God with all your heart and with all your soul and with all your might." (Deuteronomy 6:4-5)

This well-known section of Scripture is known as the Shema, which is, interestingly, the very first word in the prayer. *Shema* literally means to listen, but in Hebrew the concept of hearing and doing are intricately linked. To listen is to act upon what the listener is hearing.

The Shema was a prayer in one sense but also a declaration of who Israel's God was; it was a statement of praise and devotion. Alongside other passages in the Torah, (Deuteronomy 11:13-21; Numbers 15:7-41) these lines from Deuteronomy were prayed morning and evening as part of Jewish daily prayer. It is customary in Jewish culture for a person to cover their eyes with their right hand while reciting the Shema, allowing for total focus on Yahweh alone. Their heart, soul and strength are drawn to the Creator — with no distractions and with total devotion to the one true God of Israel. With this forming a huge part of daily ritual, it isn't surprising that Jesus used the Shema to sum up the Torah. Loving God with your entire being and perfectly loving others fulfills the law. (Matthew 22:36-40) In short, the Shema is a daily prayer, a declaration of love that moves beyond "lip service" and ritual — that calls us to truly listen, hear and act accordingly.

07.
NORA TATINA

"For you are a people holy to the LORD your God. The LORD your God has chosen you to be a people for his treasured possession, out of all the peoples who are on the face of the earth." (Deuteronomy 7:6)

In this verse God erased every doubt of the origin of Israel's identity and replaced it with confidence in His sovereign choice. He reminded them of who they were — chosen, treasured and exclusively His. Not only were they chosen by God, but they were hand-picked *"out of all the peoples"* on earth to be His and to be holy; God distinguished between Israel and everyone else, declaring His people were to be uniquely different. This distinction is crucial because it adds weight to why the Israelites were not allowed to intermarry and why God commanded that they completely destroy their enemies and the altars of the pagan gods. (Deuteronomy 7:1-6) Israel couldn't afford to allow anything to divert their devotion from the living God, the One who had chosen, loved and redeemed them. For Israel to live in light of who they were, they were to live differently — as chosen people!

08.

KAYLA FERRIS

"See, I have set before you today life and good, death and evil." (Deuteronomy 30:15)

In the very beginning of time, God set a tree in the garden of Eden called *"the tree of the knowledge of good and evil"* (Genesis 2:17). Adam and Eve were told not to eat from it, and yet the serpent tempted them by saying a taste would make them *"like God, knowing good and evil"* (Genesis 3:5). The words *"knowledge"* and *"knowing"* mean wisdom that comes from **experience**. In other words, the moment Adam and Eve ate from this tree, everyone born from that time forward would experience the effects of both good and evil, life and death.

We certainly feel this today. And while many of these experiences are out of our control, the Lord reminds His people that some are in our control. In Deuteronomy 30:19-20, He says to *"choose life"* by loving the Lord, obeying His voice and holding fast to Him. In this world, we will experience the effects of both good and evil, but we can choose how we will walk through that experience. Jesus came that we might *"have life and have it abundantly"* (John 10:10). And best of all, for those of us who have chosen to place our trust in Jesus, forever life and eternal goodness are ours. (John 3:16)

09.

CHERYL DALE

"And these words that I command you today shall be on your heart. You shall teach them diligently to your children, and shall talk of them when you sit in your house, and when you walk by the way, and when you lie down, and when you rise." (Deuteronomy 6:6-7)

If ever there was a time in history to prove the critical importance of God's instruction in Deuteronomy 6:6-7, it is now. Even back in the time of Moses, it was evident that God's people are susceptible to the influence of the sinful world. Only by staying God-focused would His people be able to resist the temptations of the pagan-inhabited land they were entering. God made it clear that reading or hearing the Word once was not enough. It had to be emblazoned on their hearts. It had to be taught. It had to be talked about often (*"when you sit ... and when you walk ... and when you lie down, and when you rise"*). Scripture is never a one-and-done thing. It's like clothing: It must be put on daily if it is to do what it is meant to do — encourage, protect, guide, rescue and comfort as it points us to Christ.

10.

CHRISTY MOORE

"And now, Israel, what does the Lord your God require of you, but to fear the Lord your God, to walk in all his ways, to love him, to serve the Lord your God with all your heart and with all your soul, and to keep the commandments and statutes of the Lord, which I am commanding you today for your good?" (Deuteronomy 10:12-13)

In the previous chapters, Moses unpacked God's plan for recovering the Israelites after their rebellion at Mount Sinai. He dealt with the sin issues, established a priesthood and provided the new tablets of the law. Then Israel was in a position to move forward into the promised land. In these verses, Moses was having a heart-to-heart with the new generation, revealing the nonnegotiables the Lord required from them:

- That their hearts would be careful not to offend Him (*"fear the Lord"*) but would make a decision to set their love toward Him.
- That they would be willing to be of service to Him.
- That they would take possession of the Lord's words (*"statutes"*), guarding them in their hearts.

This call for love and obedience requires an expression of vulnerability, faith and hope in the Lord. *"Love bears all things, believes all things, hopes all things, endures all things."* (1 Corinthians 13:7) God's people in the Old Testament, and His Church today, must trust every command the Lord has is for our good even if we cannot understand it. The Lord has plans for our good, and not for evil, to give His people a future and hope. (Jeremiah 29:11)

Notes

Notes

Notes

Notes

Notes

Notes

Notes

Notes

Notes

Notes

Notes

Notes

Notes

Notes

Notes

Notes

Notes

Notes

Notes

Notes

Notes

Notes

Notes

Notes

Notes

Notes

Notes

End *Notes*

"THESE ARE THE WORDS": WHO WROTE DEUTERONOMY?

[1] Thompson, J. A. *Deuteronomy: An Introduction & Commentary.* Inter-Varsity Press, 1974. p. 47.

STRUCTURE AND FORM IN DEUTERONOMY

[1] Patton, Matthew H. "Week 1: Overview." *Deuteronomy: A 12-Week Study.* Crossway Books, 2015.

[2] Stewart, Don. "Why Do Some People Reject the Idea That Moses Wrote the First Five Books of The Old Testament?" *Blue Letter Bible*, https://www.blueletterbible.org/faq/don_stewart/don_stewart_679.cfm.

[3] Block, Daniel I. *Deuteronomy.* Zondervan, 2012. p. 28.

[4] Lucas, Ernest. "Covenant, Treaty, and Prophecy." *The Gospel Coalition*, https://www.thegospelcoalition.org/themelios/article/covenant-treaty-and-prophecy/.

DAY 5

[1] Block, Daniel I. *Deuteronomy.* Zondervan, 2012. p. 132.

DAY 6

[1] Block, Daniel I. *Deuteronomy.* Zondervan, 2012. p. 169-170.

[2] Block, Daniel I. *Deuteronomy.* Zondervan, 2012. p. 176.

DAY 7

[1] Mackie, Tim. "What is the Shema?" *The Bible Project*, 2018, https://bibleproject.com/blog/what-is-the-shema/

DAY 9

[1] Block, Daniel I. *Deuteronomy.* Zondervan, 2012. p. 232.

DAY 21

[1] Gill, John. "Commentary on Deuteronomy 21." *Gill's Exposition of the Entire Bible,* 1999. https://www.studylight.org/commentaries/eng/geb/deuteronomy-21.html.

DAY 23

[1] Flemming, Donald C. "Commentary on Deuteronomy 23." *Fleming's Bridgeway Bible Commentary.* https://studylight.org/commentaries/eng/bbc/deuteronomy-23.html. 2005.

DAY 24

[1] Spurgeon, Charles. "The War of Truth- Exodus 17." *Spurgeon's Verse Expositions of the Bible,* 1857, https://studylight.org/commentaries/eng/spe/exodus-17

DAY 26

[1] Meek, Russ. "The Suzerain Vassal Treaty (Covenant) in the Old Testament." October 14, 2020. https://russmeek.com/2020/10/the-suzerain-vassal-treaty-in-the-old-testament

DAY 34

[1] Gill, John. "Commentary on Deuteronomy 33." *Gill's Exposition of the Entire Bible,* 1999. https://www.studylight.org/commentaries/eng/geb/deuteronomy-33.html.

DAY 35

[1] "Mount Nebo." *Encyclopedia of the Bible,* Biblegateway. https://www.biblegateway.com/resources/encyclopedia-of-the-bible/Mount-Nebo

[2] Gill, John. "Commentary on Deuteronomy 34." *Gill's Exposition of the Entire Bible,* 1999, https://studylight.org/commentaries/eng/geb/deuteronomy-34

About *Proverbs 31* Ministries

She is clothed with strength and dignity;
she can laugh at the days to come.

PROVERBS 31:25

Proverbs 31 Ministries is a nondenominational, nonprofit Christian ministry that seeks to lead women into a personal relationship with Christ. With Proverbs 31:10-31 as a guide, Proverbs 31 Ministries reaches women in the middle of their busy days through free devotions, podcast episodes, speaking events, conferences, resources, Online Bible Studies and training in the call to write, speak and lead others.

We are real women offering real-life solutions to those striving to maintain life's balance, in spite of today's hectic pace and cultural pull away from godly principles.

Wherever a woman may be on her spiritual journey, Proverbs 31 Ministries exists to be a trusted friend who understands the challenges she faces and walks by her side, encouraging her as she walks toward the heart of God.

Visit us online today at proverbs31.org!

PROVERBS 31
ministries